COTTAGE AVENUE

By Dorene Johnson

© copyright Dorene Johnson written 1995

All right reserved. No part of this book may be reproduced in any form or by any means electronic or mechanical including photocopy, recording, or any information storage and retrieval system without permission in writing from the publisher.

ISBN 978-0-578-12204-5

FUZZ PUBLISHING

DEDICATION

To my wonderful family and Deanna, Gayle, Gwen and Janice

DISCLAIMER

There are many who read this that will disagree with what I have said and with my perspective. I hope you will realize that this is how I remember it as a child and further how I felt as an adult. It may or may not be exactly as it happened. But we know that life is a personal, continuous event that unfolds in our eyes. I find that aspect of life so fascinating. We all see things so differently.

If I have offended anyone I apologize. If you get just one chuckle, I am gratified. If you shed a tear, I will know you have lived some part of this story.

INTRODUCTION

Here I am on an airplane to Reno, Nevada with three other non-stop talkers; Gayle, Deanna and Janice. Three of my very best friends in the whole world. We are headed for the fifth friend's "Castle". Yes a castle. We are not sure how she acquired this castle but we are about to find out.

I have not seen the friend in Reno for about 20 years. Seems strange. I have not seen the others much more except for Deanna. She and I have become two lonely divorced women who have always had much in common, but now our lives have once again evolved to the same status. It seems when you marry and have kids you kind of go off in another direction and it isn't until everyone is gone (including your husband) that you start thinking about the people who really count. They count more than that husband that you gave so much to. They fill lonely times between the fleeting hours you have with your own children. They understand you and hear what you say.

So it is that the five of us once again found ourselves gathering, and why so much of my life has surfaced to make me want to write down all that is on my mind.

It is hot in Reno. It is July, 1993. Leaving the plane and coming face to face with each other, all five together was a melting of 35 years. We could have been 18 again and we had just called the gang together for a slumber party.

How did we get to here? My mind started whirring as the stories unfolded and the heartache and happiness of all the years spilled from all of us. How can so much happen and yet nothing. Every one of us, except Gayle, has been divorced and some of us twice.

But even Gayle was overflowing with all the same things we have been harboring for years.

And so it was that we went to the castle, and I started my memory trek back to try and capture why I am who I am, and what has made these five people so important to me.

This is also a story about a small town and its evolution in my mind from the fairyland existence I remember, to the reality I now know.

Part I

CHAPTER 1

REFLECTIONS

Cottage Avenue is a street, like none I have seen so far to this point in my life. But I have not traveled that much, so maybe someday it will appear again. In your town it probably is called "Main Street", for on its way through town it comes to the one block business section.

The beginning of this unique street was an old narrow concrete bridge. Modern engineers have widened it since, in the name of progress. Wider cars, more traffic and all the excuses we always hear when change is in the wind. The bridge had narrow walkways and concrete railings which housed light posts with the traditional white round bulbs that can be seen for miles but don't seem to shed any light on the immediate area. Under the bridge rushed a very fast, glacier fed river that from the time of my first memory. I was warned not to go near for fear I would be sucked in and swept to certain death. This is a very frightening thing to tell a child but I have to confess it did impress me. However, through the years it did not keep me from disobeying and seeking the excitement of standing on the banks.

Cottage Avenue was typical of the whole little town. In the summer when the heat seemed to pour down on the earth and even the dust found it hard to rise when you stomped on it, the street was cool and inviting. Huge maple trees with enormous leaves bordered both sides and made the walk enjoyable. In the fall these same trees shed their leaves and I would shuffle through the ankle deep sea, listening to the rustling sound and smelling the odor of green decaying vegetation. Winter I would trudge through high piles of snow shoveled to the side of the walk by residents along the way. It didn't occur to me to walk on the cleaned off path. It was more fun to slip and slide and become exhausted by the weight of the winter clothes mother made me wear to stay warm. I was so accustomed to traveling the wet hard way that I was made to wear my boots long after others had put them aside for the spring. I never could pass up a puddle. Again, it would be summer and the full leaves would be out. It was almost like walking through a tunnel.

At the lower end of the avenue was a little park that when I first knew it, housed a grandstand that drew people every Friday night to hear the community band. As parks go, it was not particularly spectacular, but I thought it was very special. After all it was the only park I had and besides it had a drinking fountain. What little child can pass up a drinking fountain? My mother always told me, "Don't drink out of public fountains. They are full of germs". I can honestly say when opportunity was given, I drank. What could possibly be wrong with anything as cool and inviting as water spurting up and out, there for the taking.

Houses on Cottage Ave. were not houses, they were people and personalities. They were all very neat. None of the things we see now on streets. No waste paper in the gutters, no lawns unmowed, no peeling paints. Everyone on the block cared about their home. Maybe that is the answer. They had a home not a house. No aluminum cans then. What a blessing.

Farther on up the street was a church. Stone and very quaint. Just the kind you would expect to see there. It was Episcopal, and since we were staunch Methodists I never had the opportunity to become acquainted. It did bother me though, for I have a curious nature and wanted to sneak inside. But like a lot of mysteries of my youth, I did not because God was watching me and he might forgive the drinking fountain, but to disrespect his house of worship – that was something else.

Across the street from this church was the local funeral home. I always hurried past, kind of looking back over my shoulder for fear of what might expel from the place. The man (who seemed very old) that owned it at the time, was actually very nice and probably in his fifties. In fact I found out years later that during the war years (WWII) when male help was scarce, mother, who was very good at first aid, used to go on ambulance calls with him. Had I known this at the time, I probably would have been fearful of her as well.

At the end of this block was the garage in which my father spent 16 long years as the bookkeeper/manager. The two men that owned the garage were brothers. The one who forced his affections on me was called "Dutch". I vaguely remember my father stiffening in his presence. I knew there was something about this man that no one liked. What I have learned since was that he was not regarded as a very trustworthy person and did not treat his wife and children with respect. Sort of a "shady character". He eventually contracted TB and was sent off to a sanitarium which was the custom. In his absence the atmosphere at the garage seemed to be happy. The other brother whom we called Uncle Charlie and his wife Aunty Joe (Josephine), I truly loved and had many wonderful times together. Across from the garage was the original blacksmith shop which had become a machine shop. The proprietor was a small man with much the same description as would fit "Pa Kettle". He wore overhauls and stood a little slumped. I found years later that his wife was a very tall woman. Stood head and shoulders over him. They had one child, a boy, who was very large and had a high squeaky voice. I wondered where that little voice came from in that big huge man.

The shop itself was quite good sized and every square inch of it was covered with spare parts off of something and every spare part was covered with a thick layer of black grease. The kind that is so mixed with dust that it makes everything look fuzzy. The windows were so dirty and smudged you could see neither in nor out and the proprietor himself must have been covered with that same grease except for the spot under the small black hat he wore. Today, if I drove by the spot where his shop had been, even though it is now the fire station, I certainly would think of grease.

The reminder of the one block business section was made up of the usual J. C. Penny store, two drug stores, one on either side of the street (Sim's Drug and Cashmere Drug), two grocery stores, one on either side (Safeway and Simpson's) three taverns, all on the same side, (The Club, Pastime and what is now Barney's. I can't remember the old name), two barber shops, one on either side, (The Royal and the other escapes me), two hardware stores, same side (Spear's was one), a cleaners (owned and operated by Gus Stavros who spoke broken English and had long dirty fingernails), small restaurants, 1 think three, (Cashmere Café owned by a wonderful Greek family, Shipley's and the Alley Kitchen), a couple of other clothing stores and on opposite ends of the block two theaters. One was very attractive and functioning (Vale Theater) and the other was an old has been (The Royal) which stood empty, except for the occasional vandal who's curiosity got the best of him and it would be rumored that someone had been inside again! A small radio station occupied what used to be the ticket booth and presented very home spun programming. Upstairs over this theater were some apartments which were not considered very nice. I was never up there so who knows. Sometimes my parents told me things to keep me from investigating. I vaguely remember the tisk from mother when mentioning those who lived there.

At the end of the street and truly the end of Cottage Avenue --- for you had to turn there and it became the highway that wound its way over the railroad tracks and out of town --- stood the bank, a very sparse little grocery store, the post office and a building which housed on the top floor, apartments, street floor our doctors office and my uncles law office, and in the basement with windows below the street a kind of down under type of restaurant. I never really liked this place for the doctor was a stern looking man who always held your arm very tightly and who always looked as though his diagnoses was fatal.

The post office was a dark drab place with what seemed like lots of old men and smelled like an oil mop. There were several barred windows with crabby people behind them. It really didn't hold much glamour for a small child. Really when you think about it the post office of today hasn't changed much. No bars on the windows, but the old men still hang out there and they have replaced the wood floors with dirty tile. Progress.

The bank was on the end of the block which made a T shape on the main street and for many years I lived with the assumption that children were not allowed to enter. The few times my dad took me inside was enough. It was very dark with potted palms and standing ashtrays with sand in them. Everyone was very quiet almost as though they were conducting a funeral in the back room and we must get in and out before we were noticed. It smelled of cigars and the people that worked there always seemed as though they were serving out a sentence. I still cannot figure out how those potted plants ever survived in that atmosphere. No doubt it was not as dark as I imagined. Every evening a janitor would and still is out in front of the bank polishing the brass plate which reads "Bank". I'm sure it is not the same man all these years but he does the chore with the same enthusiasm.

That was Cottage Avenue as I remember.

On March 7, 1937, mother went to the St. Anthony's Hospital in Wenatchee, a town 10 miles away, to have me (attended, I might add, by the same Dr. Thompson who for so many years squeezed my arm and soothed my wounds). My name was to be Robert Mark but when I arrived I did not come equipped to carry the title so ended up just plain Dorene. My sister, four years my senior, was just plain Geraldine. She was born in Leavenworth on a very cold January 12th and mother always told how she almost froze to death in that awful hospital. So when it was my turn we went the other direction. Our plain names have for years been troublesome; no middle name. Even today when you say that you have no middle initial they look at you with that ---sure, it must be an awful name to lie about. The truth is mother was born Dora Grace Ella Christensen and then added Johnson. No wonder she was determined that no child of hers would carry a handle like that. And we didn't.

Mother was Danish. Her parents had come from Denmark and traveled across the United States in a covered wagon and eventually homesteaded in what is now Greenwood, BC. She came from a large family – being the youngest. Grandpa Christensen died before I was born but I came to know Grandma and love her dearly many years later. Father's parents lived and my father grew up in a little town called Chewelah in north east Washington. Grandma Johnson died when I was about four, but from the things mother told me about her, she must have been a very fine woman. Grandfather lived to 98. The story of him is in itself a book. They were mostly Norwegian. You might say we were Scandinavians and although we did not live by strict Norsky rule, we had certain bits of tradition. Enough to give our life a little color and connection with the past. And so it was that I came into the world and began my journey.

CHAPTER 2

THE AWAKENING

For some reason summer always comes to mind first. I like summer. It has always represented freedom, warmth, fun, casualness, and all the things connected with being rather irresponsible. My memory is vividly imprinted with the lazy feeling of summer. It somehow feels as though it comes from the inside out until you look up and see that hot glaring sun beating down on you.

My first conscious thoughts are of that summer feeling. We lived at the time of my birth in a small stucco house on Cottage Avenue. Our family always named our houses. It was easier to trace our steps that way. The Little Stucco House was just that. A glistening tan stucco that to this day has never been painted. Maybe it wasn't supposed to be as some clever contractor had put chips of shinny something in the stucco. It seemed at the time that it was a very big house but as we all know things are very different through the eyes of a child.

The house had a basement which was only accessible by an outside stairway which descended from beside the back door. They were nice stairs as I can remember well spending what seemed like hours following mother up and down as she carried each load of washing to the line to hang.

At this point, I was not very aware of my sister but do remember she had a fascinating pet rabbit. The family, as a rabbit patrol unit, was to move the furry ball at intervals to a new shady spot. It was tethered in the backyard. But as families will, everyone had more on their mind than the poor rabbit and consequently it had a sun stroke and died. My first encounter with death. What an awful reality that not only was the rabbit dead but life was very fragile. My sister was devastated. I do remember that and for years after either by guilt or sadness for the poor animal the rabbit story never seemed to quit. Someone always had to remember and go over the details.

We lived next door to a very nice older woman whom we have always referred to as Grandma Miller. Isn't it wonderful that this woman we still remember even after all these years? If, in my lifetime someone remembers me with endearing thoughts, long after I am gone I will feel as though I have lived for something.

Sometimes Grandma Miller took care of us for short periods of time but mostly we just liked to go to her house and see what was there. Compared to our house it was huge. Gray siding outside and gray atmosphere inside. It was one of those places that even with the lights on it was gray. The upstairs of this house had never been finished but there was a stairway with a door at the bottom. When you opened the door a window at the landing let a stream of light fill the stairs and illuminate a wicker baby buggy parked at the side of the window. My family were church people and somehow I thought this was surely God's light embracing me.

As with most people trying to entertain children, Grandma Miller was prone to giving treats. A very good way to distract young ones. However, the treats were very unusual. We would be given bologna sandwiches and coffee. I was so amazed that mother was upset when she was told of our diet. It was delicious. Mother did not believe in store bought lunchmeat. Nothing like that was ever served at home. Mother never said a word to Grandma Miller because it would hurt her feelings. Another early lesson. Always consider others. Grandma Miller was a gray haired blur. Maybe that was because everything in her life seemed gray.

I shall never as long as I live forget the time Grandma Miller's dog bit me. It sounds strange but it was in self defense. If you have ever had an anesthetic and are just coming out from under you will know how I felt that day. It was a though someone else was in charge of my arms and legs and I had no control at all. Poor old Shep was a really nice dog but for some reason I was compelled to go over and eat out of his dish while he was trying to eat. Not sure what was on the menu that fascinated me so but I do recall that as a last resort to save his meal he bit me on the hind end. Many apologies ensued on both sides and my fear of dogs took root.

Of all my memories of this house I only remember mother as a no faced figure but on this day I found for the first time that there was something of importance in her that so mechanically dealt with everyday life. She was so disgusted with me, or maybe even more with herself. How could this happen in such a civilized household. Easy. I was a child! She picked me up, Grandma Miller grabbed the dog. "Oh, Mrs. Miller, I am so sorry. Please don't blame the dog", she apologized to Grandma Miller. And for me a swift retreat to the House with on-going retorts of, "What on earth were you doing?" "You know better than to do a thing like that. Nasty, dirty, dog dish. Shame on you. Poor Shep. What must Grandma Miller think?"

Hayden House

Some time elapses in my memory, and I recall finding myself living in the Hayden House. It too was on Cottage Avenue. This house was a seemingly large house (bigger than the Little Stucco). You know the vintage. Gray shingle siding clear to the ground with a large high front porch that housed a swing suspended from the ceiling. Nice built in railings one could walk on if not caught. There was also a straight back, as we would call it today Deacon's Bench on another side. I remember dad taking us out on the porch on a hot summer evening and swinging with us. He introduced us (my sister and me) to thunder and lightning on that porch. It was a fact that if it started to storm we headed for the porch. Didn't want to miss a minute of the magnificent lightning and thunder! Because we lived in the northwest this act was probably semi safe. For people who live where storms are severe it was an act of foolishness. Whatever, the conclusion is, I have never feared lightning and thunder. There is a very good reason for the show of a storm. Maybe it is to watch. This is not to say that I wasn't frightened. I was very timid. But dad was there protecting me and I just nestled under his arm and made the best of it. Hot sticky nights on the porch under his arm.

The Hayden house had two big trees out in the front lawn. Maples of course. The back yard was probably the best place of all. It had a row of fruit trees on one side. There was an apricot, cherry, plum and peach. I spent a good part of our play time with my sister under those trees. We had roads in the dirt in which we drove our little cars that dad brought home from the garage. He worked for a Ford dealer and they gave away replicas of their latest models. I think they were piggy banks. In years since I have shuttered to think they were all thrown away. Today antique dealers would probably find them interesting.

The haven of dirt, worms and ants was also our very best mud pie baking spot. We baked such delicacies that we often found ourselves eating some of them. Only a child's mind could imagine a mud pie into something worth eating.

Inside the house seemed huge to me. Brick fireplace at the end of the living room with glass enclosed bookcases on either side. The dining room was large also and housed a huge table and chairs. One wall had build-in cupboards and drawers with a window seat on which I could sit and look out to a field of clover where on warm summer nights all the neighborhood kids would play hide and seek.

The kitchen was large also. It had the old fashioned built in breakfast nook with a high back bench on one side and chairs on the other. A door opened from this area which led up stairs to the attic. I always wanted to go up the stairs. However, the attic was not finished and I was told that should I go up and step between the two by fours I would fall through the ceiling. Wow! What a fragile house. I can only suspect that my parents by this time were very much aware of my curiosity and the only way to curb it was by fear. They did take me up to the attic to show me the danger. There was sawdust for insulation and I envisioned being suffocated in this endless pile of sawdust. Possibly two inches thick?

The back porch was all glassed in and a very cheery place. Our room (my sister's and mine) at that point was a good sized room with a door to the bathroom and on through the bathroom to mom and dad's room. Their room was off limits. We could pass through or visit but there was no loitering. By now you should realize that my personality dictated that if it was a no, I had to figure out how to do it.

Dr. Hayden had build the house and then died. But for convenience he had cut a hole between the living room and the bedroom to house the telephone. A curtain divided the smartly designed opening. We did not know about cordless phones or multiple phone calls then so really this was an ingenious idea and also a very intriguing one. For me anyway I could spend lots of time playing with the black very heavy phone and curtain. No doubt I spoke to many operators. You know the ladies that sat at a huge board filled with plugs attached to cords and said "number please". Mom was always shooing me away.

There was a cloak closet across from the phone and like most houses in those days it had a window high up on the wall. I used to spend time in there because the family camera was sitting on a shelf in the closet. My presence there was proven when the pictures were developed and there were several of the window and ceiling that I snapped.

Cashmere was about 1,000 people. Rentals at that time were scarce and unless you knew someone who knew someone it was almost impossible to find a place to live. The school district was bringing in some new women teachers. That was unusual for those days as most teachers were just there or so it seemed. Probably all the men teachers had gone to war. Where would these two new single women live? Now you must remember it was different then. Respectable women didn't just live anywhere they felt like. Alone, God forbid!

I can remember the low conversations between mom and dad but until it was announced that we were to have a teacher live with us I really was not that aware of what was happening. Probably too busy taking pictures.

That was when the cheery back porch became my sister's and my bedroom. Bunk beds installed and oh how I loved that room. It was the best thing that could happen to me. New Chenille bedspreads. I had to sleep on the bottom which was an insult but when you spent as much time as I did sleep walking it was the safest way to precede.

Maxine, one of the teachers, would be given mom and dad's room and they moved to our room. And then she moved in one day. Only a person of her qualities and concern would have stayed past the first day. What an adventure as they brought in all her things and I began my mental analysis of just what I was going to investigate first. She was a whirl wind of energy. Everything was in its place and straight. I watched every article being properly folded or hung and put away.

One item of immense interest was a set of fencing irons. Maxine was a physical education teacher. The irons were directed to the front room cloak closet. Oh my. The adventure of sitting looking and feeling those irons when I had no idea what you did with them overcame me. But alas, mother as usual took action and I was forbidden to enter closet. As a child we all think our parents don't see us. We are invisible. Not mom. I was very visible and didn't seem to get away with much.

Maxine was a short, somewhat stocky woman. She moved with an efficiency and speed that was only exceeded by Mary Poppins. Every task that was hers seemed to vanish with little effort. Dishes disappeared, beds were made post haste, dinner table set. No fooling around. What I didn't know was that Maxine grew up on a wheat farm in Pomeroy. Eastern Washington has a lot of farm land. Work was a way of life and the sooner you did it the sooner you were able to do other things. A concept to that point I had never been aware. Probably because I hadn't really had to do any work but would start finding out because Maxine was happy, fun loving and everything you could want, but no one didn't do their share. Under her direction I soon was assigned drying dishes. I'm sure her policy was "If you are going to hang around, you are going to work". And I did.

She soon became a very good part of our lives. She loved children and devoted a lot of her spare time to my sister and me. She played with us in the evenings and was of course a great help to our mother. She always made our chores fun. She also was guilty, according to mother, of getting me too "would up" before bed and consequently I couldn't settle down and sleep. But it was fun. All except the nightmares that ensued. I don't remember what they consisted of but I do remember waking up screaming.

At the end of her first year's stay we were very sad to find she was going home for the summer to help on the farm but as summers have a way of filling up with fun things even though you don't seem to do much, so did that one.

There were no children my age in the neighborhood. I soon fell into the habit of going everywhere and doing everything with my sister. She became a person to me for the first time. She was a very imaginative child, four years my senior. She also had a spell over me that I could never seem to control. Geraldine could talk me into things that afterward I would realize I was out of my mind to do, but never the less she had said to do it, so I did.

On our side of the street lived a girl named Laverne. As I recall she was a year younger than my sister and across from her lived a girl whose name was Bea. She was a year older than my sister and I am sure did not appreciate having me around but was always very gracious about it. Either that or I was oblivious to any innuendo that may have come my way.
Bea, Laverne and my sister were together much of the time. I was always tagging along. Whatever it was that we were doing escapes me for the most part except for the occasional time that I was allowed to go to the town swimming pool with them and of course the hide and seek nights.

Going to the swimming pool in the afternoon always included a treat on the way home and I remember an early event which included stopping at the drug store and my sister deciding we would have chocolate ice cream cones. More likely I insisted and threw a fit but anyway that was what was purchased. For a nickel, I might add at Sim's Drug. By the time we had walked the block and a half home in the sweltering heat, I had chocolate ice cream from one end of me to the other. The mess is still vivid in my memory. Sticky brown chocolate. Of course my concern was not for my clothes but for the fact that I had not been able to eat fast enough to save it. My sister got into so much trouble. Another instance of mother venting her frustration of an imperfect situation with, "You should not have bought her such a messy treat. I probably won't be able to get the stains out of her clothes".

There were those times when I was left to myself. Precious times for my sister I'm sure. One in particular I think of so often. As Cottage Avenue was also the main highway through town and the state for that matter, all the big trucks and tankers ground their way past our house daily. They were immense and the oil tankers made a special impression on me. They were green and had a snout on them that contained the engine and this whole structure took on the look of an alligator. Or at least in my mind. What was it I said about my sister having an imagination? It ran in the family. Oh well. When I would hear and see one of these immense creatures approaching I would race for home as the front porch was safety and you must reach there before it overtook you. The fear of that approaching vehicle and loud noise inspired a great flow of adrenalin. If I had not started soon enough and found that it was impossible to reach the porch, I would fling myself face down on the sidewalk and lay there breathless until it had passed, heart beating so hard. Can you imagine the laugh the driver had seeing this wild frenzy as he passed?

Sitting on the side of the house facing the vacant lot in which the clover grew untouched and wondering just what it was that made our next door neighbor, Mr. Carlton grow such funny cucumbers was one of my pastimes. Why Mrs. Carlton was such a mysterious figure was another thing I pondered. I would often crawl under the bushes and watch the ants run in and out of the honeysuckle trumpets, or lay with my nose to the grass and watch the world beneath my feet come alive with bugs and worms. I found out much later that Mrs. Carlton was not a well woman and did not leave the house much and when she did I was sure it was to put a hex on someone. Judge Carlton, her husband and the town's municipal judge, always raised a huge garden and give mother various varieties of cucumbers to make pickles. To me there was only one kind of cucumber and it wasn't those.

On balmy summer evenings we would round up all the kids we could find and play hide and seek in the clover patch. The smell of the clover was so sweet. Also there was an ever present shiver up my back because I was notorious for having to go to the bathroom immediately upon the start of any play. You didn't go to the house to get relief because first of all you would miss something going on outside and then there was the fear that mom would tell me I better just stay in and get ready for bed. So---you endured.

In the Hayden house we had many family back yard picnics and was probably one of my first conscious contacts with some of my relatives.

CHAPTER 3

FAMILY

(This part you may want to skip over as other people's families may not interest you. However it was part of my formed personality.)

THE JOHNSON FAMILY

Dad's family consisted of four brothers and four sisters. Aunty Stella and Uncle Leon (dad's sister) lived in Cashmere. They had two sons LeRoy and Duane. I really did not know LeRoy till years later as he had gone off to war. Duane was my idol and if he showed up at any family gathering I was in heaven. Aunt Emma and Uncle Jake (dad's sister) came with their adopted son Don. (We called him Donnie.) He was of course spoiled and pampered because they could not have any children and Don was everything to them. A red haired, fair skinned boy. Aunt Margaret and Uncle Walt (dad's brother) had two children Roger who was about Duane's age (10 years my senior) and who could have done nicely without family gatherings and often did, and Gretchen who was a year younger than me and very timid and I thought of her as a little fairy. She was so sweet and shy. Aunt Ethel and Uncle Carl (dad's sister) were from Chicago. They had two children Bob and Valdine. Now because a good Norwegian family always uses names over and over, I had an Aunt Valdine also. So—we called Little Valdine just that. What a handle. But we must keep them straight. When she matured someone, probably herself went to Val. These cousins were from a different world. One of money and indulgence. Bob, I can honestly say I never knew. He didn't come with them that I was aware of and Val was rather shy and who wouldn't be, having to enter our world and survive. Uncle Bill (dad's brother) and Aunt Martha had three girls. Kay Korene and Elaine. They did not always come to these affairs. Not too sure why but they seemed to have more struggles than the rest of us so possibly it was harder to come when beckoned. Kay was aloof, Korene a whiner and Elaine a baby. Again, I really did not know Kay that well. She was a year older, Korene a year younger, Val was also a year younger. Again no one my age.

Aunt Vesta and Uncle Clark (dad's oldest brother) had no children of theirs but both had children by previous marriages, none of which I was aware of until I grew older. Last but not least was Aunt Valdine and Uncle Martin (dad's youngest sister). She was the same age as cousin LeRoy. They eventually had one child Judy much younger than me and the same age as LeRoy's oldest girl. This is far too complicated and to a child even worse. I lived from one family get together to another always collecting small bits of knowledge as to how I fit into the picture. I really never felt a part of those events. I was always a different age from the rest and I felt set apart. I am sure no one else thought of it but it was there with me.

When the group was at our house (always summer) there was a large round table brought from somewhere to the back yard and wood chairs that were always freshly painted with yet another color. By the end of the picnic season chips in the paint would reveal the past year's colors.

I never had a relationship with any of my cousins until we all became so old that we could not remember who was oldest and youngest. I liked Gretchen but she was so timid and afraid that I would become bored because she would not play with me. There was Donnie whom I liked to feel was under my supervision. He was smart as a whip and always managed to get me into trouble. I didn't enjoy these affairs. We were taught to be nice to everyone and like everyone but sometimes it doesn't work out, especially when you are so young. I was always glad when the last slobbery kiss was given and they all left.

Please keep in mind all of you relatives who read this that these feelings were as a child. There is no way at that age that you can appreciate all of the personalities and the wonderful love and affection that comes with the whole scope. I really like myself to a dog in that I only lived for the moment.

We went to Chewelah for some family get-togethers in the early years. Picnics on the side lawn which was referred to as "the orchard". I have been told that we went for Christmas but I do not remember. The only thing I remember is going in the summer. Playing in the hammock and having picnics. However, I will say that probably most of the memories I think I have are stimulated by pictures I have seen. I do remember the house seeming very large and Grandma Johnson in the kitchen making pea soup, which I hated. I also remember Grandpa Johnson making me eat hot cereal which I am sure I threw up. I also remember drying dishes. We slept on the back porch in a great huge feather bed no matter the weather. I also remember going when Grandma was dying. I really did not know that was why. She was in bed in a small room and she always wanted me to come and give me a hug and kiss. I was not fond of her as she had whiskers on her face and they pricked. When she died and we came back for the funeral I remember not feeling bad that she was gone as I would not have to kiss her anymore. How awful!

One other thing I remember about going to Chewelah was going to Aunt Emma and Uncle Jake's house. She had a set of Fiesta dishes in every color and I thought it was wonderful to eat off such beautiful dishes. Also there was a creek flowing through their yard. (More water to play in.) I remember begging Aunt Emma to sing and after much coaxing she always sang a very over-stated rendition of "Way Down Upon the Suwannee River". No doubt she had a horrible voice. She had big eyes that sparkled when she did fun things.

The CHRISTENSEN FAMILY

This group of people are a little fuzzy. I have been told that Grandma Christensen came to stay with us for a while when we lived in the Hayden House. I do not remember. Grandpa Christensen died in about 1934-35 before my time. I have seen pictures of him and heard stories of how he died a pauper because he was always giving needier people his money. He originally made a lot of money after homesteading in Boundary County, BC. Mom told of having servants and how they were the first family in the area to have a car.

Mom was the youngest in the family. I do not know the order of birth but it was something like this: Uncle Andrew who lived in the U.S. (Eugene, OR) and had two boys Thomas and Albert. Uncle Albert who was married to Aunt Nellie. They lived in Portland and had Al (Albert) Larry, Glen and David. We knew both of these families about the best because they lived near and after Uncle Andrew's wife was gone (where I don't know) he came at least once a year. Aunt Annie who married Fred Hopkins and they had Gwen, Freda and raised Ronnie who years later I found out was Gwen's illegitimate child and the orneriest kid you could imagine. Gwen was about as old as my mother – a few years younger. There was Mary who died shortly after having Ethel the same year that my mother was born. Mom and Ethel were raised by Grandpa and Grandma and were like sisters. At

27

this point do you get the idea that I am my own grandpa? It isn't over yet. There was Edward who died saving all of us in WWI. That was the war just before the "Great War". There was Eli who died in a mill accident in Oregon somewhere. Another person I have only heard about. There was Aunt Martha who married Albert Hopkins (Fred's brother) and they had Leona, Betty, Alice and Albert. Now if you are confused about all the Fred's and Albert's join the club. We called one Albert, Alby, Bert, Fred, Alfred, Freddie and if I was to name all the kids of kids it would continue on. There was also a brother Fred who married Vi who the few times we tried to visit them, Vi hid. They had Margaret and I honestly do not know who else. We did not have much contact with them. I can't imagine why!

About the only contact I had with these people was when we went to Canada in the summer and everyone would meet at a lake. Shirley, Alice's daughter had a son my age, Danny. I vaguely remember him. Aunt Annie and Uncle Fred used to come to our home and visit and we would go to theirs. They were funny people because Uncle Fred was an engineer for the Trail Smelter. He and Annie had spent years in England until the war and then he was sent to Canada to make metal for the war effort. The smelter was kept very secure and I can remember at their house, which was across the street from the smelter, had guards and a high fence. I was told not to touch the fence because an alarm would go off.

Don't know if I ever set it off or not. I do remember their house had a bear rug which was a big draw for me. The head had its mouth open and looked very fierce. I was basically frightened of it but could not leave it alone.

When Aunt Annie and Uncle Fred came to our house we laughed a lot and they were such devoted people (to one another that is).

Every morning of their married life they took turns bringing the other one tea in bed. Can you imagine having a man bring you tea or coffee in bed? It is no wonder I have such fairy tale ideas about marriage! I had all these role models who were absolutely nothing that I have ever come in contact. Where are you Uncle Fred? I remember he had a car that was some foreign thing that he dusted every morning and every winter he took the motor out of it and cleaned and re-whatever you do to a motor to make it better. Drove it for years at 35 mph.

Aunt Martha and Uncle Bert never came because they were too poor. I seem to have a lot of relatives on both sides that used that excuse for being antisocial. It really did not matter as I was very busy with my own life and these visits always interrupted the business at hand.

Now that I have gone over the multitude of relatives I must introduce some people who were early in our lives and very important.

CHAPTER 4

FRIENDS

GRACE AND ROYAL

I'm told that this childless couple lived behind us when I was born (The Stucco House). I don't remember that. What I do remember is that they came to our house frequently and at first took my sister on little day trips. What was happening was Royal owned the first slot machines, nickelodeons, punch boards, etc. in the entire eastern part of the state. They were very wealthy by our standards and very close friends of mom and dad. They drove a huge Packard car and Gracie had large diamond and sapphire rings and wore the most beautiful mink and whatever fur coats. I can remember my first thoughts were to run up to her and pet the coat. Royal was tall and thin and talked a lot. Always was full of stories that everyone laughed at and I did not understand. (Later in life, much later, I found out they were what my folks would call 'shady stories'.) Mom and dad did a lot of things with them and when I got old enough, I got to go on some of their trips to collect money from the machines. It was such a treat to go to a restaurant and sit up to a counter, which mom and dad would never have done, and order anything I wanted. I remember the time I ordered liver and onions. I hate liver and Gracie knew it, but she let me order anyway. Of course I did not eat it. Royal always ordered big bowls of ice cream with some kind of topping and then would proceed to stir in it. Now mother never allowed stirring in anything. I do believe mom felt Royal was a bad influence on us but never made mention. Until mother died, Grace and Royal spent Christmas Eve with us. It was tradition. I can remember the excitement of their arrival as they always brought us the most wonderful gifts. They always took us for a ride to look at all the Christmas lights around town and when we returned Santa had just been there. We continued the tradition for the grandchildren until they were too old. We were in touch with them until Royal died in about 1993 bent over and still telling dirty stories. Gracie died several years later.

Grace and Royal's home wherever it was, was always so beautiful. They had the very most expensive things. I used to want to go to their house just to gawk. Gracie gave us her old shoes for play. She had such small feet that we could almost fill them.

What wonderful times when the old shoes arrived.

Gracie was very short and had very long hair which she braided and wound around her head several times. (Never changed.) Her laugh was special and whenever I think of her I can hear it just as plain as if she were beside me. It is one of those things that I hear every once and a while. I can't explain. It was so happy.

AUNTY JOE AND UNCLE CHARLIE

Uncle Charlie was one of the brothers that owned the garage where dad worked. He was a very rotund man with a very large nose. Cauliflower so to speak. Wonderfully kind and always called me Puggins. Aunty Joe was a small woman who was very determined in her approach to anything and everything. She liked to talk a lot and Uncle Charlie liked to tell stories and while telling them he would laugh until the tears came. They had no children either and so they also spent Christmas Eve with us. We sometimes stayed with them when mom and dad had to go out of town and their house was so very different from ours that I was always eager to explore. I think it was the fact that it was untouched by grimy hands and was more of an adult world. We were of course not allowed to handle things at home but seeing other people's things was a treat. The only thing about Aunty Joe that I know I worried about was food. She was used to cooking for two and I was sure I would not get enough to eat. Never happened. Uncle Charlie always had a new car (of course he did they owned the Ford Garage). It was a big treat to get to go in their car because we had a 1936 Ford and as dad was very conservative we did not get a new car (used) until 1946. Uncle Charlie liked chocolates and often he would bring out a new box of the most wonderful assortment of candies. I can remember being urged to choose quickly which was agony. You could only have one.

I guess you can see that my folks were the hub a lot of entertaining. Our whole life we never seemed to lose anyone, we just added to the crowd.

CHAPTER 5

HAYDEN HOUSE REVISITED

As always, fall set in and all my attentions would be centered around the basement. We had what seemed like a very large basement with all kinds of good things to do. Many small rooms, nooks and crannies to explore. My sister was back in school and I would be left again to follow mother's every move. There were clothes to be hung outside which mother carried up through a stairway trap door that went directly outside from the basement. This same door was where we threw the kindling that was delivered from the local mill. We had a trash burner in the kitchen and when it got cool we would get a load of wood to burn. My sister and I were suppose to throw this wood down the basement and I detested the job because I always got splinters in my hands and would have to have them all pulled out. There was also the inescapable fact that I would have pitch all over me and in my hair and mother would have to work on me from head to foot to get me suitable for entering the house. As an adult I have fallen into wondering why on earth would a parent set a child to such a task knowing they would be the ones to suffer. As a parent I was guilty of doing the same thing over and over because I was sure it was building character in my own girls.

The basement had one large room with a fruit room off to the left and on the right was the wood room and further down the furnace and sawdust bin. For those of you who are too young to know what a sawdust bin is, we had a furnace that burned sawdust. The local mill delivered this by-product to almost everyone in town. Nowadays they make pressed boards out of the sawdust. At the very end of the basement was an area which was filled with the belongings of the doctor that owned the house. Or I should say used to own the house, for he was dead. There was an old iron bed, phonograph (crank type) and a large dresser with many drawers and doors that we (my sister and I) loved to look through.

We were not to go into this area because of the obvious. These were not our things and they were being stored there by the family and we should show respect by not intruding. Yah sure. If we had known what neon signs were, they would have been flashing in that space just for us. Here it is kids; come explore.

We loved to play the phonograph. Lots of wonderful old records far beyond our musical savvy but fun to listen. If I am trusting my knowledge of myself I would say we jumped on the bed. Or maybe I jumped on the bed. My sister swears she never did any of those things!

Evenings and weekends my sister, whatever neighbor kids were let out, and I would roller skate in the basement. We also had a bunch of old clothes that we could dress up in and always the bed ghoul would ruin our fun and we would have to stop for another day.

When the snow started to fly we were outside again. Wow that stuff is wonderful.

We lived about 4 years in the Hayden House. During those years WWII started and the beginning of a somewhat different kind of life although I really was not that aware. My folks were rather conservative people anyway so most of the cut backs in food and supplies really went over my head.

As kids we didn't have new toys for Christmas. There weren't any. It was always someone else's hand me down that dad had repainted and fixed. And no one else had anything any different so I was very happy with whatever I got. There were no tricycles or bicycles or dolls or buggies. But we always seemed to have it all. The only hurtful thing I can remember was the fact that I never got a scooter or pedal car. I have harbored that rejection for years, so much so that I made my kids have both and they never rode the scooter, but they did have miles of fun in the peddle car. I am joking of course. The only thing that I feel is the love of my parents to try so hard to give us those precious toys and the hours of labor to make it the best it could be. It is interesting to think back to those times especially knowing what I know now about WWII, that somehow through all the uncertainty and doing without I can never remember feeling afraid. Somehow my parents were able to instill in us confidence and faith that the things we did, that were directly related to the war, were only a part of our life. We did them because it was the way we lived and not for any special reason. However, I might add that we didn't have TV and we only listened to the radio when the folks turned it on. Much different than today.

During the war years mother had to work. Not because we needed the money but because other people needed the help. In the fall she would go out every day and pick apples. I can remember getting up very early and going out while there was still a heavy frost on the ground. If we were lucky it was only dew. Those were long days for me. The only thing that made it all worthwhile was that we packed our lunch and got to picnic in the orchard. Mother also worked for a friend who operated a grocery store. He needed checkers and they had to be women. That coupled with the ambulance calls she did for the local funeral home, life was interesting. My dad was too old to go to the army. A blessing or a curse I never knew. A blessing certainly for us.

I can remember our home being opened to service men that were being transported across the country. They were some of the nicest men. My first exposure to different accents from different parts of the country. One fellow was from Texas and we were mesmerized by him. Mom spent the day in the kitchen because she would try to make them whatever food they most wanted. Within reason of course as variety of food was limited. Choices were made and she would bake.

This house had its share of sickness. My sister and I had a bad case of hard measles. A seemingly long period of time of soda baths and lying in a dark room that had purple crepe paper covers over the lamps so our eyes would not be ruined. We also contracted poison oak for the first of many times. You would think that after a while a person would recognize what the plant looked like, but alas no. Life started to take on a shape for me here in this haven called the Hayden House. Feelings of warmth, community, family and responsibility were beginning to govern my life.

Besides Bea and Laverne there was Janet and David. They lived across the street from each other on Cottage Avenue, but about four blocks from me. This was definitely not an allowed walk so time spent was at a premium. Prearranged so to speak. Janet was to become a good and loyal friend a few years later and constant companion. And there was David. He was my boy friend, playmate and brother all rolled into one, and I might add a dear friend.

Uncle Andrew first came from Portland for Easter while we were in this house. At that point in my life I didn't know much about mom's family except that they talked different. (They all had grown up in Canada and never seemed to lose some of the inflection.) Uncle Andrew's wife had departed. As it was in those days, you didn't talk about things that were unpleasant. Just ignore and maybe it will go away.

Andrew's two sons, Tommy and Alby, did not surface till I was a little older and for the moment I only was enthralled with Uncle Andrew. He gave me money. Small coins. I really did not get my hands on money back then and a nickel was like a million. What a decision to make on how to spend.

Easter was the beginning of spring for mom. It did not matter if it was early or late we had certain things that did not happen until Easter. For instance, no one who was fashion conscience wore patent leather before Easter. You did not break out cotton linen anything until Easter. It was the same in the fall. September 1 you got out the wool. Oh how I hate WOOL. It is a wonderful material for those whose skin can tolerate, but for me it was a curse. Wool did and still does cause me such discomfort. My mother could not understand that I had sensitive skin. The wool went on anyway -- after all how were you to keep warm. And keeping warm was mother's most fervent concern. Back then they thought you got colds from drafts and flu was something you just happened to run into. I had to wear long stockings made of wool. The crying and arguments that ensued prior to the donning of these garments finally wore my mother out at about age 6. She finally got it through her head that I was truly miserable.

There are many wonderful memories from the Hayden House. The big overstuffed rocking chair that mom and I would sit in and rock. Sunday night supper in front of the fireplace and getting to eat on a card table. Lots of family there always sitting around visiting and sometimes playing games. Sounds strange by our standards. No TV. Only our own devices to entertain. It was during these years that some of dad's coworkers at the garage where he worked would all get together. There was Aunty Joe and Uncle Charlie, Gig and Stella Helgerson and their son Russell. Russell was so much fun because he would play doctor with us. Sounds perverted but it was harmless. He was a very fun loving person and was more than patient with my sister and me. It was in this setting that my dad first let me sit on his lap and drive the car into the narrow garage. It always seemed very late (probably 9:30 p.m.).

All the gatherings at our house started with dinner around the big dining room table.

There was Maxine – she was part of our family, Christmas, making Valentines and May baskets in the kitchen breakfast nook, crawling all over the mohair davenport that tickled your legs, feeling the steam coming from the hot registers and I guess in simple words just a warm happy feeling. Knowing you were loved very much and you had security and plenty.

I was deathly afraid of dogs. Probably because of the nip that old Shep had given me. Whatever the reason, I became hysterical whenever a dog got too close and so the doctor prescribed a cure. Get a dog!

So ---- enter dog. It was suppose to be a Cocker Spaniel, but it turned out to be a Heinz. It was golden brown in color so we named it Penny.

Penny was a wild completely undisciplined dog that I know mother felt like killing. Whatever you hung on the clothesline it tore down. The clean clothes mother had hung out, our tents came down as fast as we put them up and worst of all mom's silk stockings. This was very traumatic as silk was unavailable to the masses because the government was making parachutes for war out of all they could get. At that time Japan was the major silk producer and as we were at war with them --- no silk. So stockings were unavailable. It was not until after WWII that nylon was invented. (Who knows when it was invented. If things were like now the FDA probably had to test it for years before releasing it to the general public.)

I was scared to death of this dog for a long time but eventually the doctor's cure did take effect and I was to have my whole life, a dog.

CHAPTER 6

THE CASHMERE METHODIST EPISCOPAL CHURCH

I cannot go any farther without interjecting the church. When I was baptized in the church it was called Methodist Episcopal, then it changed to just plain Methodist and then years later when it merged with United Brethren it became United Methodist, which it is today.

We HAD to go to Sunday School and every so often church. It was the feeling that you had to get used to going to church and sitting quiet for an hour. Boy were they wrong. I still can't sit for church service quiet and content. Anyway, we were big church goers. Mom always belonged to a "Circle" and they were always cleaning the church, the parsonage (minister's house provided by the church) or making quilts or cooking some big meal. I spent hours touring every nook and cranny of that building and it was a big one.

At Christmas we always had pageantry, including old bathrobes for costumes (Sheppard), sheets draped over a wire that was collapsing in the middle and old sandals that were too big. We had parts to play and verses to memorize and recite. The only teacher I remember was an old woman who was considered an "old maid". Ada Jones was her name and I can picture her gray hair pulled back in a bun and glasses. Severe clothes and nature. Really not a lot of fun to have for a teacher. In my mind kind of grumpy. I am not sure she liked kids.

Our church family was of course Aunty Stella and Uncle Leon, Grace and Clark Bixler, The Larses, Durlands, Grandma Dronen, McKellers, Zedikers (Gwen's family) and I could go on and on. Lots I have for the moment forgotten.

There were the Padfields, J.L and I believe Esther. He always carried a bible with him and we were constantly reminded that they had lost a son in the war (that's WWII). I believe his name was Kirk. Anyway there was a plaque in the entry way of the church with the names of those lost in the war.

The building itself was a very large, red brick with many gables and many many rooms all done in dark wood but with lots of those little square windows. A beautiful sanctuary with a huge vaulted ceiling and two balconies. The sanctuary is a place that I can sit or kneel and hear the voices of those who have put so much into the continuance of the church. Lots of those people I only vaguely remember but we always talked about as though they were still present. Dad in particular never let go of a friend. With him they lived forever. After they died he would go to the cemetery every year and clean up their graves and put flowers. Each year the task grew. Sometimes it took a whole week.

Our church was the largest building in town and we had all the important things happen there. Baccalaureate for the high school funerals of large size regardless of denomination and large weddings. A structure to be proud. I was baptized, became a member, married, baptized both of my children, and buried both of my parents --- all in that church. I will never as long as I live lose the feeling I have when I think of it.

The six years that we were involved in WWII starting 1941, possibly set the pace for a continued simple life style. Had the war not happened, with the coming out of the depression, we would have gone on to a more materialistic way of living.

I was four when Pearl Harbor happened. It wasn't until I was grown that I found out that Pearl Harbor was a place rather than a "happening".

CHAPTER 7

THE APARTMENT

This perfect world of mine was suddenly to come to an end when our parents told us we were going to have to move. They had tried to buy the Hayden House but the real estate agent had sold it to someone else who had given them just a little more money. It was a very low blow to my folks and it consequently upset us all for we had to move and there was no place to move. Worst of all it was the first encounter in my life of letting go of something I loved. Our dog. The folks took an apartment which was all they could find on such short notice but I complicated the problem by coming down with Whooping Cough just as we were going to move. This is a disease that has been for most of the world obliterated. Thank goodness. I can remember being taken to Aunty Stella and Uncle Leon's and coughing and vomiting until even as a child I wished to die. I really can remember the feeling of please God release me from this horror. Someone kept vigil at my bed night and day and I vaguely remember the different ones that would be wiping my brow and talking to me.

When I finally came through the illness I was moved to the apartment. It was right in the middle of down town Cashmere up over the Cashmere Café Restaurant.

Maxine even moved to the apartment with another teacher, Ruth. A different one but she was just down the hall. We were in this apartment for about a year. It was a difficult year for the whole family. It was my first year in school. Aunty Stella had to take me the first day of school because my folks had to go Canada because grandma Christensen was ill. I was so afraid to go to school and so upset that mother was gone that I made Aunty Stella stay with me until noon. I had never felt so timid in my life. I don't think my folks realized either how lacking in self confidence I was. It didn't help matters any that during my first year of school my sister and I had Scarlet Fever, I had pneumonia and probably wasn't real healthy when I started from the bout with Whooping Cough. We were quarantined, which was the practice, and dad had to stay at Aunty Stella's because he had to go to work. What a way to live. I don't know how mother stood the year.

In spite of my illness I passed the first grade. I was a smart child and did well up until about the fifth grade. It was then that I realized I could get B's without studying and what else could anyone want from me.

The apartment experience had some good points. I remember a small balcony overlooking the alley where I would sit with my feet dangling over the edge. I remember being let go down stairs to the restaurant to get soup. They made wonderful soup. I can remember getting to spend much more time at Aunty Stella and Uncle Leon's. They were such warm and wonderful people. Aunty Stella had a little lilting laugh that I can still hear. She had twinkling eyes and large breasts that when I sat on her lap became a pillow. She was kind and I could be in her presence for hours and never feel unwanted or a pest which I am sure I was.

One of the things that happened about this time, and I really am not sure just when, but Maxine became engaged to her long time sweetheart and I think got married that summer. At any rate she moved back to Pomeroy. However, this was not the end of our relationship My sister, being older, was first to get to go to the farm. Max and Ellis had a large wheat ranch down in the Pomeroy area and we spent several summers enjoying "ranch life".

Then of course there was Duane. The love of my life. He was very handsome, thin and knew all the ways to make me thrill to his presence. Riding on the handle bars of his bicycle, taking me to the show and just paying attention to me. He had a bedroom downstairs that was forbidden territory. When Aunty Stella was mad at him for over sleeping or possibly other things I knew nothing about, she would send me down to his room to bug him. I was a master at it and the thought of entering that room where there were model airplanes and sailboats and lots of boy stuff. Wow! He of course was always gracious and usually gathered me up and gave me a big kiss. He still does. It is one of the memories I truly cherish. Can it be that God will someday allow us to live this simple life of joy again?

Aunty Stella and Uncle Leon's house seemed big, of course. It had the most wonderful back yard with a hammock in one corner that we put excessive miles on and wore out the grass underneath. We jumped off the back porch to see how far out we could land. The house in reality was very small but we always had large family gatherings there.

Summer in the back yard, winter inside. The dining room was very small but somehow everyone was seated. Aunty Stella was a marvelous cook. I spent hours watching her make glamorous dishes, or so I thought, and I remember she had an ironing board that came out of the wall. Sometimes she would let me iron the hankies. At both Aunty Stella's and at home ironing was a big job. EVERYTHING was ironed. I can still smell the fresh smell of everything as it was being smoothed and folded. I still like to iron. Crazy I know, but I do.

Aunty Stella did not own or want an electric mixer. She beat everything by hand! It was fascinating to watch. And the most amazing part was the results she produced from this very high energy activity. Aunty Stella made peanut butter and honey sandwiches, could slice fruit to make you think it was something different, kept an immaculate house and always wore a dress. Of course, so did mom. She was never too busy to talk to me or care for me. She was the most wonderful person. Gray hair that was almost white, full figure, mid- height, beautiful face and very stately.

Now you may wonder about their other son LeRoy. The truth is I never really knew LeRoy until I was about 10. He was off to war, (WWII) shortly after my arrival and all I knew of him during those years was when a letter would come and we would all gather around and Aunty Stella would read it out loud and cry. At that point in my life I really had no idea who he was or why everyone was crying.

Uncle Leon was the learned attorney who had an office just about a block away. He walked to work every day, as we all did, and came home for lunch every day, and took a nap after lunch every day, then walked back. He had dark hair, medium build and wore glasses with small dark rims. I always thought he looked like Bob Hope. He had a work bench in the basement where he tinkered. I spent a lot of time watching the tinkering. One of the things we always laughed about was the putting up of the Christmas tree. Aunty Stella was never satisfied with the tree as it came. Soooooo, Uncle Leon had to always add limbs and it was a very nasty process as he would add the ones she wanted, and then when he got it up she would decide she needed another somewhere else. Amazing process as at our home the tree went up and dad said that tinsel was made to fill the holes!

I don't remember if we moved in the spring or summer but everyone was excited because dad had secured a house for us. We had all gone to look at it and I was so ready for this move. It was to be on South Douglas which was just one block off Cottage Avenue. The first time in my life I had not lived on "The Street", and I was seven. But there was a real drawing card with this house. Janet lived just one block away, and across the street from her was David.

SCHOOL

I guess I have kind of skimmed over school. I did not get to go to Kindergarten as the public school did not have one and the only lady who offered private quit for some reason. (Probably after having my sister she gave up, Ha!) Anyway I went straight to first grade. You remember the day I would not let Aunty Stella go home.

I had a very nice teacher but for some reason I was afraid of everything. Afraid to answer questions, afraid of putting the wrong thing on my papers, afraid to color out of the lines. And besides that I was sick with all those diseases. At any rate somehow I made it quite well and was passed on to the second grade. Now this is where trauma really started and I feel that it followed me for some years until I reached high school. I was placed in a new teacher's room. Her name was Mrs. Blackwood. I can still see that woman. She was, to me, very tall and chewed her nails all the time. She was obsessed with having us read fast. OUT LOUD - IN FRONT OF THE CLASS. And if you did not read as fast as she thought you should she beat your hands with a ruler until they were red. Now mind you, I read very fast and never had my hands beat but I do remember some who didn't and the trauma of having to watch the beatings was awful. Poor Everett was her whipping boy. He got whacked almost every day. I was so afraid of that woman I even wet my pants in her class. I was afraid to ask to go. Well, as it turned out some of the parents finally listened to their kids and it was discovered that this woman was using the supply closet to drink alcohol all day. The damage was done. I do believe it was the reason I did not enjoy reading until much later in life.

Third grade I had another great teacher. Miss Lavesser. She was kind and even tempered and I am sure knew the story of our previous year. I, as usual sailed through this year with good grades and felt more comfortable about school.

Fourth grade I had Marta Brooks. She was to be a lifetime friend but at that time I did not know it. She was probably the best teacher I have ever had in my whole life. She recognized my shyness and really helped me to come out of my shell. Also my friendships with Deanna, Gayle, Janice and Gwen were flourishing and they were a great support group. We all were for each other.

Fifth grade took a nose dive again. I had Mrs. Osborne. Gwen and I both got stuck in her class. She was a skinny dark, harried woman who stood at the back of the room and then when she chose to come up behind you came with such a flurry and noise it scared you to death. I again was traumatized with actions. I remember she was obsessed with making us appreciate music. There is nothing wrong with that, but she played the "Hall of the Mountain King" over and over and asked us questions about it until I didn't think I would ever get that melody out of my brain. We had several kids that had been held back with us from the previous year, and I remember feeling sorry for them because they were having trouble with school anyway and then to be put in this nutty woman's class was unthinking.

MOM

I don't really think, up to this point, that I had much of an insight to mother. I took her for granted. In reality, mom was about 5'3", trim figure but not skinny. She had naturally curly hair that was just there, always looked the same. How I envied her never having to work at having her hair nice. She <u>always</u> took a bath around 4:00 p.m. and got "cleaned up" as she called it for the return of dad from work. She at this time would also sit down and have tea. If it was summer would have a pitcher of lemonade or iced tea with some cookies, and other times hot tea and treats. Then she would start dinner. This procedure never changed. I didn't realize it at the time but she was very fashionable. Always had beautiful clothes and looked great. As I reflect now, I know that she taught through her actions more than anyone I have ever known. She was a doer of things. Never just talked about them. She always had a cause and many of them were people. She provided a home that was neat and clean, cooked, washed, gardened and was fresh when dad came home, just like nothing had happened. A stark contrast to my years of looking frazzled and irritable at dinner time.

DAD

R. E. Johnson, who had dark hair, brown eyes, about 5'8" was very skinny and was in his own way just as structured as mom. Every day was a white shirt, tie and suit. Polished shoes; winter – overcoat & hat. He walked to work and back and also walked home for lunch. Everything had to be painted. But, the catch was that he always painted in his white shirts! I didn't really realize this until I was older. Mom used to get so irritated because he would get flecks of different colors of paint on his good clothes and she could not get it out. Dad's answer to hurts and aches was to rub the damaged area. Maybe he wasn't too far off since circulation is a key to healing. Dad loved to tease. He willfully cheated at whatever game we were playing just to see if we would notice. His appetite for hiking and being out of doors was with him until he died. He never met a stranger.

CHAPTER 8

BRASK HOUSE

Annie and Polly Brask (never knew his real name) owned four houses all in a row on S Douglas Street. They lived in the one next door to us. Annie was a very wiry woman, then probably in her late 60's and Polly was a retired contractor, plumber, and Jack of all trades. He had a shop out in back of their house where he tinkered. Now this man was seemingly very grumpy, short, stout and greasy. We called him Poddy. That came about because of his grandchildren and nephews who came to visit. They all called him Poddy. We had a real desire to watch what Poddy was doing in his shop and therefore his reputation of being grumpy. However, as I recall I think he spent considerable time patiently explaining many facets of the grease world.

Annie on the other hand liked to visit with everyone and walk at a very quick pace. She seemingly had little to do and often that irritated my mother who took house cleaning, washing, ironing, shopping and decorating to heart and had little time to dawdle.

It was not too long after we moved into the Brask house that mom made a mysterious trip to Wenatchee and my sister and I were not invited to go along. When she came home she invited us to look in the front seat of the car and there was the tiniest little black and white Toy Terrier dog. We were so excited. We named her Toy and she was out constant companion for years. She let us dress her up in doll clothes and run her around in the doll buggy. She was always around just watching and waiting for inclusion. She went to the lake with us and lived until I was about 15 or 16.

The Brask's had one daughter, married with two girls. One a year older than me and one two years younger. These two gals started coming to visit their grandparents and stay for extended times and our friendship grew with each summer day that first year. They fit right in with the neighborhood antics. In addition to the oldest whom I spent my time with, there was Dick who was kind of a cry baby, Kenny who was tougher than nails and was really on the fringes of legal play. There was a girl, Kenny's cousin, who for the life of me I cannot remember her name. She lived with her parents in a spooky house at the end of the street right on the river bank. They seemed to be quite a bit older than what I was used to and this little girl was either someone else's that they were raising or a late in life happening. She was not always a very compatible playmate but we included her when necessary. Mostly for those late evening kick the can adventures. Of course Janet and David lived around the end of the block on Cottage Avenue, so there was much to do at this house.

Poddy built us a play house in our back yard. This was the scene of much work and imaginative play. We would not enter it for weeks and then all of a sudden we would be inspired to clean and arrange and play for an entire day. Imagination was our forte. Between Geraldine, Margaret (David's sister), David, Janet, and anyone else who happened along we could dream up most anything. We also spent long afternoons making tents on the clothesline and sometimes sleeping there all night. Another favorite was to listen to the radio when it got dark – programs like "Inner Sanctum", "Green Hornet", "The Shadow" and other mystery radio programs and we would scare ourselves and run for the house. I can remember a couple of years dad put up a big canvas tent in the back yard and he and mom slept out there with us. My dad always loved to do things like that. We hiked every trail in the area, drove to the top of every mountain, saw all the Forest Service "Look Outs" and picnicked regularly in every known camp ground of the time. Sometimes it was in the back yard and croquet. Always big pitchers of iced tea or lemon aid.

We had a picnic box. It was metal and had all the necessary things in it to, at the spur of the moment, load up and go.

The back yard had a white picket fence around it. Couldn't you have guessed? It was the complete American dream and I can imagine none of you think that is real. It was and that is part of my absolute unreal upbringing. I cannot think of one thing in my 0-18 life that did not emulate Ward and June Clever before they ever existed. I hear all the time people making fun of that TV show but in fact it really did exist. It was not someone's imagination. I lived it!

I have failed to tell you about Douglas Street. It was a dead end street that turned off Cottage Ave. On the left hand corner lived the Ablings. You remember the man uptown with the grease place. Well there they were. Mrs. Abling was very tall and verrrrry grumpy. Of course if you had to live with Mr. Abling and Willie, I guess it was justifiable. Their yard was rather unkempt. Things were allowed to grow at will. It was an interesting place at that. Really had possibilities if someone had taken the time. On the other side of the street from Ablings was the Christian Science Church. Small white building with a vacant lot behind. This lot was on a small incline that made for great sledding in the winter. Then the rows of small houses began on both sides. Our side, the right side, as I said, Brask's owned. One was Dick's house and another was Mae and Ed's. The other side were people that I didn't know because they had no children. Why would I know them. Except for Grandma Dronen. She lived right across the street from us. There was a Mr. Dronen but he was a mere shadow. He worked all the time at the mill and what little I was around him, he smelled like sawdust. They had 11 children. Yes ELEVEN. They were all grown. Much older than me and occasionally came to visit. But you would think that out of eleven there would be a greater response to Grandma Dronen's needs. I guess they were gone or too busy. Anyway, Grandma Dronen spoke broken Norwegian and weighed 500 lbs. I am not sure of the weight but at least 350.

She was a Saint. In spite of her girth she had a small face, very small mouth, dark eyes and was always so glad to see us. Mom always did lots for her. Mr. Dronen died during those years. Since he had never played a significant part in my mind I really did not miss him. The only thing I can remember so well was my mom taking Grandma Dronen in the car and my very real fear that the car was going to tip over when she got in.

Mom and Dad never forgot Grandma Dronen even though we moved away. We always took her food and never missed a Christmas Eve visiting her. For you see she was one of God's angels. She taught me what it was to give yourself to others. It does not have to be anything much. But it must be from the heart. If she was not an angel, why would I still think of her and have such a warm feeling? When you entered her house you became instantly transformed into the most secure comfortable, almost unreal atmosphere. She would make such a fuss when mom would come over, always with some eatable treasure. She would always have coffee on and it smelled so bad because she boiled it on the stove and left it sit there all day. Mother always had a cup and never even winced.

Next door to Grandma Dronen's was Norman Bates' house. Only at that time I had never heard of Psycho. They sure could have used it to film the movie. The elderly Lawrences lived in this cluttered, gray, vine ridden mass of mystery and only came out to go to town in an old Model T. Since it was Kenny's grandparents and that other girl's we of course felt the right to investigate the grounds at will. There were never any warnings from the old folks or even any indication that they were aware of our presence in their yard. Mom had a fit if she caught me, just on general principles of the Privacy Act. At any rate we did window peeping when we could and all I ever saw was a lot of dusty furniture and bird cages. Kenny had to go over on occasion but we were never invited to enter. We did not even bother them on Halloween. Probably because we were scared of them and threatened by our parents.

Down the street past Kenny's house, which was beside ours, were several more houses that we were not suppose to go to (disreputable people no doubt) and on the end across from "that girl" was Newlands. They had two children also. A boy and girl. They were younger and we really did not play that much with them. **And then the river.** On the river bank was what we called the jungle. It was really forbidden territory. DO NOT GO TO THE JUNGLE! Hah! So guess where we sneaked off to whenever mom was gone for a few minutes.

It was a heavenly place with lots of trees and squishy ground and vines and probably snakes. The water kind that are harmless. The river was very swift but gradual on that bank and we were of course fascinated by the whole scene. I got caught there a few times and my parents would forbid me to play with Kenny because they were sure he was the one leading me astray. I don't remember but I probably was the one who led him. When Kenny was in trouble his father would beat him out back in a shed. I can remember the yelling and crying and I would cover my head and hope he was okay. He always came out looking fine. I think it was a lot of noise. He never had marks on him and never stopped doing the things he did to wind up in the shed.

At least once during the summer I would be invited to go to Annie and Poddy's granddaughter home and stay a few days. They lived in a place about 4 miles away on a big fruit orchard and I, being a city kid, thought I was in heaven. I was a world traveler and besides they lived in a beautiful house that was so far beyond even my imagination, it was such a treat. They always had bottled pop too! We had it sometimes but not on a regular basis like they did.

Those trips to the ranch were special because we roamed the whole place and found rotten eggs and threw them at whatever and took baths in a lovely tub and slept in beautifully decorated rooms. Now that is my memory. Probably wasn't as grand as I thought but it was for me a step up. As if I really needed anything to stimulate my need for nice things. Expensive things. I have never lacked good taste at least in material things. One more thing about going to the ranch was that they always had a big garden and unlike my mom and dad they grew things I had never seen before. This was my first sighting of yellow tomatoes.

My parents were very predictable. We ate the same things and fixed it the same way and we did not deviate. Tomatoes were red in their mind and so we did not grow anything but red tomatoes. That's that. My mother cooked everything until it was dead and falling apart. That was to insure that there was nothing of evil origins left and it also insured that there was no food value left. Of course we did not know that then, so that was just the way it was.

I remember a silly thing my sister and I used to do. We always wanted to shuck the fresh corn because if you took the corn silk and held it under your nose like a mustache and recited in a deep voice "You must pay the rent, You must pay the rent". Then you made a hair bow and in a high squeaky voice "I can't pay the rent, I can't pay the rent." Then in a male voice with the corn silk in bow tie position "I'll pay the rent". To cap this rendition off in a high squeaky voice with hair bow, "My hero". Now is that dumb or what? It kept us busy and mom did not have to worry about getting the corn ready to eat. (I might add that this was done outside.)

I hated steaks until I was married and found that you did not have to make shoe leather out of them.

Dad made friends with everyone. Everyone had good in them. Everyone had some quality to offer and so it was that he was fast friends with Chief Tucumsa. What we would say today a Native American. He was married to a Native American woman named Marie. When we first started going to the Chief's they lived in a two story house that had no furniture. A small table and maybe a couple of chairs. We went to this farm for the purpose of raising our huge Victory Garden. Everyone had to have a Victory Garden. We always had a small one at home but this was major in size. I am not clear as to what happened to all the produce. We grew every imaginable vegetable and lots of potatoes, and pigs. We each had a pig. The pig pen was down on Mission Creek which flowed through his property. Also at the pig pen was a very large crop of Poison Oak. I seemed to have bouts of this itchy awful condition all summer. Between that and mosquito bites, I was plagued with scratching.

We would go out to the Chief's in the evening and I can remember playing in the rows of whatever and coming home completely covered with dirt. You know the routine. Take off outside. Don't come in the house with all that dirt on you. It was great fun though, and at the end of the evening we would go to the house and Chief would perform one of his Indian songs and we would be mesmerized.

Another of dad's friends was Owen. He had a wife, Coila. Owen was a very outdoorsy person. Wiry like dad. Coila was full figured, one of those curly hair dos, and had big brown eyes. She smoked a lot and they had a Cocker Spaniel dog named Corky who was very mean. I am sure Corky was simply not used to kids and gave out warnings when his territory was invaded.

The wonderful thing about Coila and Owen was their cabin at Lake Wenatchee. During the summer we would go up to the cabin on weekends with them and then we would spend one glorious week up there by ourselves. I loved those vacations. It was the dense forest, trails to explore, swimming in the glacier lake, sleeping on the sleeping porch in all kinds of weather and cooking on a wood stove. (I am sure that was a treat for mom.) There was no electricity, no bathroom (outside) a handled pump in the kitchen, deer and bears hanging on the walls, no vacuuming or dusting. Washing dishes was exciting for several reasons: 1) not very many dishes; 2) nothing else to do when it got dark; and 3) mom was sure that in these conditions we would probably not achieve cleanliness so she mostly did the chore.

Every night when it got dark dad would get out the old pump up gas lanterns and we would play games at the long table. I have such warm feelings of that place.

My sister went several years to Camp Zanika Lache (Campfire Camp) which was just down the road from Coila and Owen's. She loved it. I went one year and never went back. I really hated all the regimentation. I was used to doing my own thing and they would not let me. They simply did not realize that I was expert at this territory and had vast experience in the woods!

Willis was also a dear friend of dad's. He was an authority on Indian Culture and actually had his own museum of Indian artifacts. This collection was given to the local Historical Society and is presently located in the Chelan County Museum at Cashmere.

Willis always took us on hikes in the woods. The only reason I somewhat enjoyed them was that mom always prepared a picnic for us and when we returned from the hot dusty adventure, she would have all the wonderful things to eat ready. Willis took dad and us kids Huckleberry picking every year. I hated berry picking and still do. I love to eat them but –oh the picking. Willis would provide Indian woven baskets for us to use. He wanted the outing to be authentic. I am sure it was. The last trek I went on was when I was about 16. Dad got me up at the crack of dawn and Willis picked us up and we went up on Stevens Pass. First we hiked what seemed like miles and then it rained. I was so cold and miserably wet that I thought the day would never end. Willis helped me get an "A" on my botany project in Biology. He brought me plants from places most of the kids had not been.

Dad was a very active person in the community. He was in the Chamber of Commerce and was president one year. He was also a staunch Democrat. I learned very early about politics and my sister and I were always having to spend evenings going door to door passing out whatever election material was available. However, there was no TV ads, no slandering of candidates and peddling papers was pretty mild, although I can remember not wanting to offend people whom I was told were Republicans. My dad never stopped being vocal about all the wonderful Democrats!

Somewhere in these years my sister and I went to Maxine's for a week in the summer. I believe I went twice and my sister at least three times maybe more. I was not a very good "go away from home person" at that time but Maxine was special so I went. We spent our week riding horses, playing in the barn which was out in the middle of a huge corral where the milk cows lived. Every time we would attempt to cross the corral I would get scared of the cows and start running. Of course the minute you run the cows think it is a fun game and chase you. Crossing the corral was very traumatic.

We spent long hours exploring all the holding pens for pigs, bulls and whatever came along. We also spent a lot of time with the old harness maker who lived in the shed away from the house. He was very patient and showed us his wares and told stories. There were chickens everywhere and my sister hated chickens as much as I feared the cows. The excitement came when chicken was on the menu and Maxine would come out and grab one and ring its neck then let it down to flop everywhere. For a city kid this was unreal.

There was a little store across the highway and down a ways from the house. We always wanted to go over there and often were sent to get a loaf of bread and of course a popsicle. It was very hot those days. The dust was lazy and tired and the walk was exhausting. But when you got the popsicle and reached home again to the wonderful trees and shade, the trip was well worth it.

Ellis would take us with him to go out in the wheat fields to inspect. The wheat was always over our heads and Ellis would carry me on his shoulders. He was a handsome man of few words but he was a loving person and father as they eventually had 6 children of their own. We did not get to go to the farm after the babies came.

Mary Lou and LeRoy got out of the army while we lived in the Brask house. They moved into the smallest house I have ever seen which was located on North Douglas just across Cottage Avenue. My curiosity about LeRoy took over and I would just happen to wander over their way and visit. Now Mary Lou was an extremely gentle person who loved children. I often took Toy in the baby buggy on the pretense of showing her the dog. She would often invite me to stay for lunch which consisted of the most wonderful sandwiches. Mary Lou has always been a good cook but she makes the best sandwiches. I was probably a nuisance to her but she always made me feel welcome. Always had time for me. LeRoy did too, but I was usually there in the day time and he was working somewhere. They did shortly thereafter move to Spokane where LeRoy entered law school at Gonzaga. This special time was the first time I had really known who they were. LeRoy was dark haired, medium height and loved to visit and tell stories. Mary Lou is short and dark haired, a little on the full figured side. She is very precise and had the ability to make even the simplest thing wonderful. You notice I used "was" for LeRoy and "is" for Mary Lou. LeRoy died quite unexpectedly in 1994. We have all missed him.

It was in the Brask house that I started the second grade and my mother let me have an overnight guest which was Deanna. She wet the bed that night. She was so embarrassed and I was my usual cool self and told her it was no biggie. I also started having sleepovers with Janet. She at my house and me at hers. They were much more frequent because she lived up the street and D lived across town.

Janet's mom had high blood pressure and was suppose to rest every afternoon. I don't think they knew about medicines then. At any rate we would always get into trouble if we were at her house because we made too much noise. Frequently we had to leave the house for outside and more freedom. The reason we got into so much trouble was a trunk of clothes. Someone had discovered the trunk in their attic and given it to Janet's folks. It was full of the most wonderful dress-up dresses you could imagine. We would get on these outfits and parade up and down

Cottage Avenue imagining we were someone or something special. The exhibitionist in me seemed to mushroom for a few years. But on the other hand maybe it was a lack of inhibition. Whatever, we had a lot of fun. We were really bad in one more thing we simply could not stop doing.

Janet's dad had purchased a lawn cart to use to haul clippings, weeds, etc. while working in the yard. It was metal and fairly sturdy except it was not designed to run road races up and down the backyard incline while one of us was riding. What fun. Every time we did this we were surprised that he knew. How did he know. The fact that it was bent and the wheels were sprung did not come into focus for us. We would get into trouble and be told not to do it again and low and behold the urge to road race would overtake us and eventually the cart was of no use to her dad and he resigned himself to "no cart". I think that is when we stopped. Mission accomplished!

Janet and I loved to spend time at David's. Margaret, David's older sister was a friend of my sister so sometimes there was just the three of us and sometimes there were five. David had a really fascinating bedroom in the basement and he did not like us girls entering. Probably his mother did not either. So it was always a challenge to see if we could worm our way into the inner sanctum of the man's world. Sometimes we made it but for the most part we were confined to the back yard where there were 2 free standing swings built on very sturdy wood pilings, one bigger than the other. I always wanted David to pump me up in the swing. He did sometimes, and they were so wonderful. I never gave it a thought but that I would marry David. He was my dream "man". I swooned over David. He was less than impressed with me and even less impressed with Janet. There were never times, without three, four or five. So you can see my relationship with David really had no opportunity. My parents occasionally had dinner at the Anderson's and so our families were friends and we just all grew up together.

I remember one time when Mr. and Mrs. Anderson were not home. Probably Margaret and Geraldine were left to "baby sit" David and me. Little did our parents know that they were not suitable to leave in charge. They had very vast imaginations and of course David and I were the victims. This time they decided that since I was the smallest I should undertake to crawl from the basement to the upstairs through the dirty clothes shoot. Sounds harmless enough. It had a crook at the bottom and one at the top. And I discovered in this adventure that I suffer from claustrophobia. With much coaxing I made it beyond the first crook and then stood up in the tube that was barely large enough for me to slither through. David was above shouting encouragement and Geraldine and Margaret were in the basement pushing on my legs when the first wave of panic overcame me. I was too short to hoist myself up to the top and did not know how to go back. Freeeeeze! Blank mind. Vacant eyes and fainting feelings. Somehow they talked me back down and out.

Of course I had gotten that far and getting back was a possibility and reality. I truly still have only feelings of panic and do not know how I got out. I think it scared all of us. We didn't engage in that kind of activity again. However, there was the day that Margaret and Geraldine told David and me we were adopted. I was so upset that I ran for home and of course the older girls got there ahead of us and tried to persuade mom to go along with the joke. She did not. But I was no longer sure who was telling the truth. The years have proven me to be so much like my sister that we would have had to both be adopted and she wasn't going to go for that.

My sister and I received our first bicycles at the Brask House. Like everything else they were someone else's fixed up. My sister got the one that was really cool. It was black and white and had a light on the front fender. Mine on the other hand was green with silver fenders and looked kind of funny because the fenders were put on lower to the back like they are today but we didn't see it as cool. I received a lot of ribbing about my funny bicycle but I could go like the wind and no one laughed at me when we were riding because I was fast. Dad clocked me at 35 mph going down Elberta hill, (or so he said). I was the king of bicycling. Janet was timid and could not keep up. My sister was the only one that was in my class. Elberta Street joined S. Douglas and it was the only way we were allowed to go to town. When we reached town via alleys, we had to leave our bikes at the garage where dad worked and walk the rest of the way. It was far too dangerous for us to ride where the cars went. I did not ride a bicycle on Cottage Avenue until I was 35!!

This process got us to the swimming pool every afternoon from June to September. My favorite place. I took swimming lessons every summer. Sometimes it was the same class over and over but I took them. I am a fish. In my previous life I was in the ocean I am sure. I become alive when I reach the shore. The only reason I don't swim as much anymore is because so much of the water is not fit to get into and swimming pools with chlorine make my dyed hair turn green! There was never a summer of my youth that I did not spend at the swimming pool.

Another part of our life was going to the show. (Movie theater, flick or whatever you call it.) We both (my sister and I) received a dollar a week that we had to buy War Savings Stamps with and when you got the book filled up your received a War Bond. We also got to go to the show Friday night or Saturday afternoon annnnnnd if you were good and did your chores and went to Sunday School maybe Sunday afternoon if the Parent Magazine said the show was fit for children. I might add that we hardly missed a change of show. It was a ritual of making the decision on Friday night or Saturday afternoon and the receiving of the twenty five cents which got you into the theater for 12 cents and you had a dime for popcorn or candy. As I watch all the old movies on American Movie Classics today I have to laugh at the fuss that was made over whether it was okay for us to go or not. Maybe that is what we need today. More restraint on kids as to what they see. The old movies have all the same elements in them but were presented with such finesse. You did not watch people go to bed, you just knew they did and so what! Everyone went to bed.

Whenever we went somewhere it was on foot. The sidewalks of Cashmere were a challenge as they were old and had cracked a lot from wintering and lack of repair. "Step on a crack and break your mother's back" was a way of life. Now it is okay to run over the cracks with your roller skates, but walking, one had to be very careful.

About once a week in the summer we would be allowed to walk up town to the Public Library which was in the upstairs of City Hall, Fire Department and Police Station combined. The Police Station had two very small cells right on the street which when it was hot (all summer long) they would leave the doors open. We were always curious to see if anyone was in there and would peer. I am sure they were drunks sleeping it off as they were seemingly in some state of non-functioning though four eyes were staring at them. It was always men. I guess women didn't do bad things then!

The library was always stuffy warm being on the second floor and the librarian was a very short, gray haired lady name Jenny Meyers. The windows were always open and when in your search for the right Nancy Drew Mystery or sometimes the Hardy Boys, you got to hot, you could go over and stand in the breath of air that was coming from outside.

Fall was a special time as we had two big Maple trees in front of the house and when the leaves fell it was heaven. We made huge houses with rooms for everything. A castle so to speak. And if we got bored with the house, we would rake up all the leaves in one big pile and jump right in the middle. I can still smell that green decaying leaf smell. Of course fall also meant Halloween.

Now dad was the person in our family who was the most inspired when it came to dressing up in costume. So when Halloween came around we got out an old suitcase which was full of old clothes and used specifically for costume parties. Dad would help us get ready and sometimes we even had a Halloween party in the basement. Corn stalks all around. Cider, bob for apples and go trick-or-treating. Real corny but true. Dad sometimes dressed up and went with us. I was usually a Devil. Never the Princess that I called myself. I don't remember what my sister depicted. When we got older and could go around the neighborhood alone we would go out and scare ourselves because it was not normal to be out after dark. The house we always liked to go to best was Mrs. Jones' who's husband was part owner of the local mill. They lived up on Elberta Street and she always gave <u>whole rolls of lifesavers.</u> That was unheard of and what a treat. Now Mrs. Abling gave us pieces of apple and told us she hoped we would get sick. Didn't go there much. Just when we really felt brave.

Those two big Maple trees also had large roots that had taken over the front lawn. One evening while we were playing hid and seek I tripped on a root and broke my arm. Mom and dad were not big on going to the doctor unless it was absolutely necessary and they determined, even though I could not move my arm, that it would be okay in the morning. Well it wasn't. By the time Dr.

Thompson got a hold of me to x-ray, major atrophy had taken hold. The setting of this arm, with no anesthetic, I might add, produced screams that my sister heard waiting in the car outside. I spent weeks with my arm taped to my side in a most unyielding fashion. It was my right arm and I am right handed. All my clothes had to be cut so I could get them on and in general it was a miserable time.

Our lives were so structured. Play, go swimming, play, go to the show, play. Listen for the Jolly Joe guy and run after him for an ice cream sandwich that only cost a nickel.

A couple of years after we were settled in our Brask House some new people entered our life. There was an alley that ran alongside of our house between Kenny's and ours. This connected another street closer to the river. In fact I believe it is called Riverfront. Anyway the house directly behind us and across another alley (every block had an alley through) was purchased by a family whose last name happened to be the same as ours and who had purchased the local bakery. They had 3 children that I knew of and two in our range. The older of the two was a boy. He was so handsome that we were always staring and giddy, I am sure, when he was around. My sister was in love with him. (We were always in love with someone especially when they were within eyesight). Unfortunately for her he was so shy that he could hardly even communicate with us let alone anything else. I am not sure that he ever married. But what do I know.

Then there was the younger sister. She was more to our caliber. Easily led by the group as she was a year younger than me and I was about the youngest. They usually only participated in the evening community games. Then through my school connection which was slowly becoming more a part of my life came Patty. Her grandmother lived up on Elberta street (the one we rode frenzied down) and her aunt lived in one of the Brask Houses. (Mae and Ed.) It was a natural for her to start visiting and enter the gang. She was very dark haired and soft spoken and extremely intelligent. However, there was a part of her that was very mischievous. Therefore, when she would ask me to come up the street to her grandmother's to play we often got into trouble.

Grandma Yenter was a very skinny fast moving little white haired woman who called it like it was. I would guess a pioneer of sorts in those times. Anyway, she had a basement full of treasures that of course we were to leave alone. What is it that the minute you tell a child to not get into something that it becomes a beacon. There was an old Victrola and I am not sure I am using the term properly because it was that kind that played the tubes. The music that was emitted from this fascinating machine was magnificent. Men and women singing operatic type renditions of things we had not heard before. Of course we usually got caught as Mrs. Yenter was not deaf nor dumb for that matter. But it was worth the chance just to hear the music.

Patty and I spent a lot of time making leaf houses in the fall. She was a different kind of playmate. Usually a one on one type person.

Our lives pretty much evolved around the calendar. Mother thought fall started on the day after Labor Day. Thanksgiving was Wednesday night and Thursday. Christmas was one week prior to December 25th and New Year's Day you took the Christmas tree down and put everything away. Winter of course started the first of November and spring began Easter Sunday. Summer started the day after school was out. We only had turkey on Thanksgiving and Christmas; ham on Easter, chicken or roast beef on Sunday and very seldom did we have pork because she thought pigs were dirty, then only washed and cooked to death.

We always had a birthday cake of your choice except that it had to have white frosting because it must be decorated. We always ate lunch and dinner together and always used cloth napkins. Dinner was served in the dining room on Sunday and for company. You never slicked up your plate. You always left some crumb so no one would think you were ill-mannered.

Now you may think that this was a very ridged way to live but actually it was great. You knew exactly where you stood at all times. No surprises. I think kids today need more of this and less soccer, baseball, etc. Today's values are so poorly defined.

We always had the same group of people for Christmas Eve. Grace and Royal, Aunty Joe and Uncle Charlie and sometimes Aunty Stella and Uncle Leon and family. Depending on the year and who was going where. We always had the exact same menu for Christmas Eve. It wasn't until years later that mother did add a few new things. Christmas Eve supper consisted of homemade white and brown bread. The white bread was made into ham sandwiches and the brown was served with cheddar cheese. Open face as mother called them. We had celery stalks, carrots, pickles and olives. We also had a molded red or green Jell-O salad and a very large array of Norwegian cookies and lefsa. The variety of cookies were Fatimans, Goro, (similar to Krumkakka) Berlina Krunsa, Spritz, sugar cookies and mother's fruit cake. Occasionally a special chocolate something. We had Mogen David wine, (dad's favorite) and of course coffee. In our house coffee was a main stay.

It was in the Brask house that we learned the war was over. I hardly knew it had been going on, but everyone else was very excited both times (VE Day and VJ Day). Everyone gathered up town to celebrate and there was much excitement. We seemed to go through the same process for the end of both Europe and

Japanese campaigns. I don't think that there was as much hoopla when the bombs were dropped on Japan. possibly because of the strong Christian faith in the community as a whole. Anyway, dad was part of the local fathers. You know the Chamber of Commerce that kind of thing. Uncle Leon was on the school board. That was really big and important. Of course he was an attorney ----- so very learned.

During the last couple of years of the war I remember we would have to listen to the radio every evening and sometimes it was an address by President Roosevelt. I can still hear his voice. I was always wanting to get on to something more fun but we were supposed to listen. Also there were news reels at the theater. Anyway when the war was over everyone was excited and I loved a good time. Dad dressed up all crazy and headed for town. I don't remember what we did that night. I was excited because I got to stay up late!

The biggest change that was to take place in our lives with the end of the war was the purchasing of material things that were non-existent for so long. I remember I had my first bubble gum. Pop was readily present in our lives for the first time. Mom and Dad would buy a whole case (bottles) and store in our basement. However, we were restricted in drinking and it was only 7-Up. I remember thinking that if I got sick maybe I could have some.

Candy bars were very scarce during the war. I guess it is because they needed them for all the children of Europe. What better thing to give a starving child than a candy bar! You have seen it a hundred times in those old movies. Well that's where they all were. All those little kids got our candy bars and rotted their teeth instead of ours. I made up for lost time however, when I finally got my hands on that wonderful chocolate.

Also mother who had been stifling her many material needs began to buy new furniture. She purchased a beautiful red oriental rug and runner for the living room and a new davenport that was green velvet. We also got a beautiful Duncan Fife dining room set and a radio with record player. We were in fat city. The Oriental rug and davenport have lives of their own which went on for years. All I can say is mother bought the best and it never died.

That Oriental rug gave me a whole new outlook on the perfection that mother demanded in our daily living. Mother usually cleaned house on Friday. You know the routine: Monday wash clothes, Tuesday iron, Wednesday go to town, Thursday bake and Friday clean house. I always hoped she would hold to that schedule because if I saw the rugs hanging on the front railing when I came home from school I knew I would not have to waste my Saturday helping. But if not, I knew I was in for a miserable Saturday. My sister and I had to dust. Probably why I hate dusting so much. I never was very good at it as mother would spot a missed place from across the room. And then there were the fringes of the rugs. They must all be lying out straight. I used to leap from rug to rug so I would not muss up the fringe. My job. Today I just lift the rug and flop it back down and it looks just the same as if I spent the time to rake through each tassel. If we cleaned house on Saturday morning we would listen to the Texaco Hour of Opera and dance around to music.

Every now and then mother would announce that we were going to Wenatchee on Saturday to shop. Now this was very special. Mother only went to the best places and we would get to eat lunch at the big hotel. We would get all dressed up in our finery and wore hats and gloves and felt great. There were only probably max 10 stores all in a row on the avenue but we would be exhausted at the end of the trek. I, of course, always wanted to go into the three dime stores to look at all the interesting notions as they were called. Junk! Mom did not let us buy anything. Just look. We had new outfits for Easter and Christmas. Mother, however, had new outfits as needed. We had to go to a special shoe store and have our feet fluorscoped so that they would not be damaged with improper shoes. Oh, they were ugly shoes. Brown for winter and white for spring. A pair of Mary Jane's for special occasions. Mom always bought shoes and purse to match. I guess her feet were already ruined. Dad liked clothes also, but he did not go to town with us. He went on his own and only shopped at one store (Mills Brother's). He always looked like a million bucks.

CHAPTER 9

BACK TO SCHOOL

What I remember most about school is the smell of that building. I know that recess was my favorite time. Always playing on the bars and showing my underwear which was a no-no. I don't think anyone ever looked at the other person. We were just doing fun things. Today the bars are probably considered dangerous but we didn't know any better. Come to think of it I never knew anyone that got hurt on our play equipment.

I never could do the monkey bars. I always fell in the middle. I hated group games and still do. So you see I was selective in who and what I wanted to include in my circle. Pretty much stuck to my own circle of friends. In the third grade Gayle and Janice moved to our town and school. That was, little did we know, the beginning of our lifelong friendship and the forming of the "Fearsome Five"; Deanna, Gayle, Janice, Gwen and myself. Gwen and I were in Sunday School together, Deanna was part of our very early years also, so things just seemed to be coming together for all of us to settle in our friendship.

Back home on Douglas street there was something brewing that I had really not given much notice. Mother was having health problems. Dr. Thompson sent her to Seattle for the purpose of seeing another doctor, a specialist, because she had a goiter. It is a condition that is virtually unheard of today. A thyroid swelling. They did not have pills then just goiters. The verdict came back from that trip, mom needed an operation. It was apparently very serious as everyone cried a lot and I was nervous thinking I might never see mom again. I remember the night before mom and dad left for Seattle for the operation. Aunty Stella and Uncle Leon had us over for dinner. Mom cried and everyone was so sad and depressed. We, of course, were left with our aunt and uncle to wonder what was happening. I must have forgotten about it shortly after they left because I really don't remember anything until the day mom came home and how careful we had to be with her. She lived through it and never had any more trouble. However, the stories of the surgery and everything "over there" were somewhat startling. How they strapped her head down and put sand bags around her so she wouldn't accidently move. All more than I cared to hear.

Douglas Street gave us a lot of very happy memories. We had many Christmases with Aunty Joe and Uncle Charlie, Grace and Royal were still spreading their joy in our lives and Aunty Stella and Uncle Leon were always close.

GERALDINE

My sister was a figure up till now that kind of led me around. The fact was and is that she had a quality of commanding all situations. She was/is very attractive. Maintained that quality that mom always had of making an outfit look good. She is a very loving kind person but has a definite way things should be done and you had better do it that way. I have a quality of avoiding confrontation, so generally went along but when I felt pushed to the edge I just disappear. Somewhat frustrating to a perfectionist and often misread as laziness. I am not lazy, just selective. There is a difference. I know I was a source of concern for my sister. Her drum and mine often got out of sync. For the most part we were together.

Geraldine had reached dating age. Wow. This was worth watching. Boys would come and pick her up for shows or dances and I was always lurking in the wings, just to get a glimpse. Now I had not seen my sister as she was. Call it preoccupation with oneself or just not paying attention. She had long dark hair, good figure, very good student, member of drill team and very popular with boys and girls. I sat up and took notice when the guys came. She had and still has a quality which I cannot define. No one had more friends, dates and general admiration. Whatever it is, I don't come close.

THE ROADSTER

It was about this time also that cousins (mom's brother's two boys) Tommy and Alby came into my life. They came to our house in the most wonderful car I had ever seen. It was an old roadster convertible. Black of course. They stayed a couple days and then left but asked if they could leave their car at our house for reasons I never knew. Of course the folks said yes.

I do not remember the timing of all of this, but I do remember the car parked on the side lawn right under the wild plum tree. We were given strict orders to stay away from the car. Green lights started flashing as usual and not only did I become involved in the trashing of this car, but so did my sister. We (Margaret, David, Geraldine and me) were in that car as often as we could get away with it, driving on fantasy trips. We would argue as to who got to drive. I remember spending a lot of time in the rumble seat but it was just great to get to go on the trips. Of course the plum tree raised a crop during this time and we proceeded to smash them in and on the car. At any rate when the boys came for the car mom and dad were amazed at the state of disarray it was in and we were in big trouble. I could never figure out why they were so oblivious to the fact that we were being so destructive, but it happened, and it sure was a lot of fun.

GRANDMA CHRISTENSEN

In about 1945 or 46, mom and dad were busy discussing a serious matter and I finally realized it involved grandmother Christensen. She apparently was very down and out and mother was very concerned. A trip was planned to go to Canada to see just what the problem could be. I only remember mother was very upset. When mom was upset everything was upset.

Mom and dad were off to Canada and we were left with a friend (Ruth Brimble the school teacher). I don't remember how many days it was but I do remember dropping her diamond ring down the furnace vent and breaking out in a cold sweat until I got the grate off and was able to hang down and rescue it. Only my sister, an accomplice as usual, was aware of this happening.

The result of the Canada trip was that mom decided that grandma should come to live with us. I will never forget the day they brought her home. A very skinny, sick, half dead person was carried to mom and dad's bedroom. The doctor was summoned and there was a lot of whispering. It seems that grandma was being kept in an awful "nursing home" if you could call it that and she was malnourished, sick from gall bladder problems and near death. Mom nursed grandma back to health with special diet and TLC. Mom and dad moved to the basement to sleep and our lives took a whole new turn.

Grandma Christensen was a character. She spoke broken English. Having come from Denmark at an early age, she never lost her accent. She had a wonderful sense of humor and she loved to dress in nice clothes.

When she gained in strength mom would invite some of the elderly ladies for tea, bought her all new clothes and she would go with us to church or whatever we were doing for the first time in a long while feeling very good about herself. It was a chance to get to know a person that otherwise was only talked about in our lives. She loved for us to play our records and there was one in particular that would make her laugh until the tears came. It was called "Ain't Nobody Here But Us Chickens". Most of the records were from Royal's nickelodeons.

Sadly grandma could only stay a year and I will never forget mom's anguish at having to take her back to Canada. They decided to take her to Vancouver, BC. Mom and dad went up and found a beautiful place for her to stay and since mom's niece lived there she felt a little better as some family could look in on her. I remember the trip up to take her and how sad it was for all of us. In one year grandma had become such a part of our lives.

Grandma slipped and fell shortly after she was taken to the nursing home and broke her hip and consequently died. It was such an awful thing for mother. The regret of having to return her to Canada and then for it to end in that way. I like to think that her life was not about slipping and falling. It was about coming to stay with us for a year that we would not have had otherwise. It is a wonderful memory.

During mom's surgery for her goiter dad met a man in the hospital. His wife was having the same surgery. Dad and Tim became friends and this man talked dad into going into business with him. Tim and Helen rented Annie Brask's house next door to us. (I don't remember where Annie had gone) but it worked out that they could rent the house with all the furniture, etc. This "creepy" man was a wheeler dealer and of course dad put up his life savings to start the phony business which I don't think lasted a year. It lasted until dad ran out of money and he finally got wise to what was happening. Dad had quit his job at the garage to do this, so when he realized what had happened he was totally broke. I can remember wondering if we were going to eat and what was going to happen.

Many friends came to dad's rescue and helped him get out from under the mess. One of them was Everett. He put dad to work in his orchard so we could eat and dad found a man in Dryden (5 miles up the highway) who was wanting to insert into the community a new modern grocery store and was willing to build a building for this purpose. One catch to all of this. We would have to move to Dryden.

I can still remember that sinking feeling. Move from Cashmere? Move from my friends? No more tents, roller skating, birthday parties, kick the can with Janice, Janet, David and Deanna? I was really depressed and feeling that life would never be the same again.

Mom and dad convinced my sister and me it would be good. We would start a whole new life in a new place and it would be great. Yah Sure! I think mom and dad were at that point just trying to escape the feelings of shame that had come over them. We were to move in December 1947.

CHAPTER 10

DRYDEN

The building we were to occupy was built along the highway but the highway was not finished. In fact it was a sea of mud. So when the store opened it was not yet convenient for people to come there and of course there was no immediate trade off the highway. The structure was 100 feet long and probably half that wide. I thought it was very large. We had an apartment in one end. Small but adequate. My sister and I shared a room which was the way it had always been.

The highway was finished and opened, I believe, in the spring of the next year. In the mean time we survived on the local trade which was slow at best. We all had to work. I started out stocking shelves and sweeping floors after school and on Saturday's.

We were sent to the Dryden schools because mom and dad wanted to be a part of the community and they had been assured that they were of the best quality.

My immediate friends became Darlene and Janice. Darlene was the daughter of the man that had built the building and they lived just about half a block from us. In fact part of the pear orchard had been cleared out for the store. Janice was her cousin and lived across town.

These girls were a real pair. I had never before been confronted with two such personalities and the never ending possibilities of their fractured minds. Darlene was the youngest of three and I do believe her mother was too tired to really pay attention to what she was doing. She and Janice were frequently telling their parents they were too sick to go to school and succeeding. For me if you went to school and if you really got sick they would send you home. They also smoked in the shed out back. This place had a loft in it and the entire structure was leaning so far south that the possibility of falling down was very real. The upstairs of their house had about 4 bedrooms but no hallway. You just went from one room to the next. I had never seen anything like it before. Darlene's house was my first introduction to crocheting. Darlene's mother must have spent every waking hour when she wasn't cooking in the kitchen, crocheting. There were fancy dolls, doilies, tablecloths, fancy pillows, wall hangings, you name it, everywhere. Mother was appalled. She hated things like that and we had none of it anywhere.

We soon became aware when we tried to enter the community of Dryden that we were of another world. Mother was a crystal and silver person and they were plastic and paper plates. Now I am not saying that one is better than the other, just that they do not mix and every time mom and dad tried to participate they were rejected.

Dad was a man that if I haven't told you before, got up every morning and put on a long sleeved dress shirt and tie and wore dress pants and proceeded to do whatever, even if it was to paint the house. I am not kidding. We always laughed because dad painted in his white dress shirts. Also, dad painted everything. He called it freshening up things. Everything he owned had little smatterings of color on them. Mother was a person who never wore a pair of slacks unless we were going on a picnic in the woods. You can see the picture. It just did not compute in a community of farmers. They all assumed that anyone that looked like my parents thought they were better than them. Not true.

I started school at Dryden halfway through the fifth grade. This school was so small that there were two grades in one room. I think my class had about eight in it and the sixth grade had about six.

My only base teacher the year and a half I was there was Mrs. Evans who was the Superintendent's wife. She was a stiff woman who dressed very nicely and my folks became friends with them for a while because they were not really accepted either. I was not comfortable with Mrs. Evans and especially when we would go to their house for dinner and then I would have to see her at school. I can't say she was bad to me but it was just a feeling. We had one hour of the day that a man by the name of Mr. Lever was our teacher. He drove a Model something A or T car that had no glass in any of the windows. He drove from Wenatchee every day and was of course the brunt of many jokes. In the winter he would be all bundled up with hats, scarves wrapped around his head and one of those black and checked, what the folks called a "Mackinaw". Strange man but he was teaching us kind of a world affairs class and I really looked forward to his time.

It was at Dryden that I played tennis and learned to play back lot baseball. I have never been a sport player. But when in Rome do as the Romans do. Of course no one ever wanted me on their team but since there were so few kids they could not overlook me.

When the highway opened the store started to get very busy. Especially when summer and fall came. Summer all the people going to Lake Wenatchee would stop and get their groceries for the cabin and fall all the fruit workers came. I learned to be a checker of groceries at age 11 and learned the grocery and dry goods business from top to bottom. Dad was very innovative and had everything in the store that you could possibly need. Even underwear and socks. Jeans and shirts. Groceries and pots and pans. Drug store sundries and lanterns. When school was out in the summer I always started my swimming lessons. The only pool was still at Cashmere where I had always gone, so I would do lessons all morning swim all afternoon and then when I got home I had to work. Slice lunchmeat, clean lettuce, stock shelves, check groceries, carry out, stock the pop machine and on and on. Lunch meat came in huge rolls and we had to slice and wrap for sale. Sometimes my sister and I would slice all day Saturday so we could go to the show or a dance later on. We worked hard but we always had everything and more than we needed. All the best clothes and the folks were generous with the car when my sister learned to drive. We had many friends who were in our home and lives.

After a year and a half of Dryden schools, mom and dad were upset. There was not all the things that they had promised. No music, preparation for college was iffy, culture was at a very low level and socially we were deprived. Sooooooo the quiet conversations started. I hated Dryden so when it was announced that we would return to Cashmere for the start of my 7th grade I was ecstatic. I can remember being with Deanna at the swimming pool and telling her I was to return. One of the best days of my life.

My sister on the other hand was very upset. She was going to be a junior in high school and was sure no one would accept her back and who would her friends be and on and on with much tears and gnashing of teeth. We went anyway and she was alone probably for a very short time and was readily accepted back into the fold. Why not? She was a very pretty girl, very smart and always popular. Actually was elected cheerleader for her senior year.

It was our Dryden years that my sister started going with Lorny. He was several years older and had money to throw around. He was not fast and loose. In fact he came from a very reserved German family and he was the heir to a small fortune in orchards. Lorny was so madly in love with my sister that there was nothing he would not do for her. He drove a blue Pontiac convertible (brand new) and I used to love to get to ride with them. He had two friends that never seemed to have or maintain dates. One was Bud and the other Bill. They were all three at our house most of the time because mother cooked meals and they loved to eat. I got to tag along lots because Bud and Bill loved a big group and also I do believe I was probably as adult or more than either. They were like my older brothers and it was a strange but fun relationship.

I can remember the night we decided to go sledding up on Hog's Back. A somewhat steep road up behind the store. We all piled into Lorny's car and Bill decided to hook his sled to the bumper of the car and ride outside up the hill. When we reached the top we stopped and got out to find the abominable snowman. He was covered with snow and frost and we could not stop laughing. This was actually a very dangerous thing to do but I guess then there certainly wasn't any traffic on the road.

We had lots of fun adventures going to shows, just cruising around in this grand car. Fortunately Lorny could afford the gas.

My sister broke his heart. He had to go into the army during the Korean War and while he was gone a parade of fellahs that would not stop made her realize it was not meant to be. Lorny often spent evenings with me after that, just to be with the family. I know he was truly never the same. I have admitted that if he had asked me to marry him I would.

As the store prospered, dad hired a man named Erle Winegate. He had previously had a store in Peshastin for years and really retired but wanted to work some. Erle was large and loved to tell funny stories about people and would laugh until the tears came. Erle became part of our family because he was such a dear person and his wife of many years became ill with cancer. Erle was not a needy person, quite able to live without employment at our store, but it became a place for him to get away to and forget for a time his troubles. He had full time help to take care of Hazel so he spent his days with us. Hazel of course died and then we became his link with sanity. He had dinner with us almost every night and we tried to keep him busy. He just couldn't go home. Erle had a pickup, I believe it was an old Chevy, probably post WWII. He kept it looking very great. Now my sister and I loved to drive that pickup. We would always volunteer for a run to the dump which involved borrowing Erle's pickup. We would be scared to death to go down across the railroad tracks where the county had established the most current landfill because it was inhabited with bums. That is not a politically correct term but we did not know we were supposed to refer to those poor people as homeless. Just bums! Anyway, I am sure they steered very clear of two teenage girls recklessly driving in an old pickup.

After about 6 months Erle was contacted by a friend of a friend and was introduced to Francis. Erle had no children but Francis did. Anyway the courtship started and we were introduced to her. She was a lovely person and we became very pleased with the possible union. It did happen and Francis came to live. She was much more outgoing and invited us to dinner and of course mom had them a lot. They were added to our Christmas Eve group. Erle was the reason that mom and dad could take some short trips and get away once and a while. Erle had a heart attack and died in the early sixties. It was one of the hardest deaths I do believe my dad endured. They were so close and had worked side by side for so many years. Francis lived for many years after but moved to Pasadena to be near her son and family. We kept in contact.

Next door to us were the Hall's. Floyd, Edna, Jean and Sybil. When we first moved there Sybil was married and her husband was in the military. Jean was in high school and friends with Geraldine. Floyd and Edna were just good people. Edna always took all the old bananas, strawberries, whatever was on the down and made some wonderful thing out of them and then would invite us over for treats. They would come to our house for dinners and coffee and were just great neighbors. In a community that didn't really like our presence, they were a breath of fresh air.

And then there was Ottie Dillenbeck. Now I have told you how mom and dad collected needy people and lots of friends. Ottie was an elderly man who had been a customer at the Ford garage for years. Dad had always done lots of favors for him. Helped him with his accounting and when his wife died he sold the farm which was way up some canyon and bought a small place in Dryden. It was a horrible little house that was not even completely finished inside. Ottie raised chickens and sold his eggs to dad, of course.

Ottie was a hair lip who had no help or surgery. It was very hard to understand him. However, after a time you caught on to his ways. He drove a Chevy coupe and was a danger on the roads. One time he almost drove into the store before he got control of the car. He most always came at dinner time and of course mom invited him to stay. I hated that. He did not make for a very good dinner partner but it was a lesson in humility.

Ottie started to fail in health and we would be sent over to his place to check on him or clean the house or bring food. He had no telephone. I can remember the day that mom, Geraldine and I went over with lots of soap, disinfectant and rubber gloves and did a complete cleaning. Mom was so aghast at the filth. From then on we paid more attention to his housekeeping and his nutrition. Ottie got sick and had to go to the hospital and guess who had to take care of the chickens? Now my sister was more afraid of the birds than I, but I confess it was not fun going into those long chicken houses that were all dusty and full of probably 200 chickens pecking at your feet. Also, there was the problem of collecting the eggs, candling them, boxing and hauling home without too much breakage. I am not sure how long this went on but the end result was that Ottie could not come home. So dad had to sell the chickens which was a tremendous relief and we had to close up the house. Ottie went to a nursing home and of course the state would not allow him to have any property so dad bought the house and told Ottie he could go back and live there whenever he was well enough. Dad did not sell the house until Ottie died. He was true to his word to him. That was dad.

CHAPTER 11

THE RETURN

I do not know why some things are so vivid in my mind. Maybe because they were so important to me at the time. But I remember my first day back at Cashmere in the seventh grade. I had shopped for all the right clothes and chose an orange corduroy skirt to wear. Tell me why I remember this?

As Dryden was not on a bus route for Cashmere School District, I started a 6 year program of riding with people who worked in Cashmere or calling mom to come and get me. I was never smart enough to date a boy who did not have sports after school so any take homes by a neat guy were out. Any way we managed.

Junior High was my first experience of having a home room and every hour going to a new class room. Boy did we feel grown up.

My most exciting and rewarding thing was my reunion with my friends, Gayle, Janice, Deanna and Gwen.

GAYLE

Gayle is a little taller than me. Not much but some. Brown hair. Round face. Pretty and I always was so envious of her hair as it was natural. Didn't have to put it up or get perms.

Gayle lived out in the Hughes addition which was a new area West of town. She had an older sister but she was several years ahead of us and I knew her but she was not around much.

Gayle's mom was the greatest. She always talked to us and seemed to understand our problems no matter how insignificant.

What I did not know at the time was that Gayle's parents were on the brink of divorce and eventually split. I am not real sure of the timing, but we were in the beginning of high school. At that point Gayle and her mother moved to town to an apartment. It was in a large house over a beauty shop. There was an enclosed stairway leading up. The apartment was not much but we seemed to gather there a lot. I think it was the atmosphere that Gayle and Lennie made. Lennie had taken a job at the drug store but it was not the popular one that the kids went to after school. Sometimes we would go there just to appease her. She could not understand why we did not frequent her fountain. It Is hard to explain that peer pressure of being in and doing the clone thing. Kids of all ages have it and still do. (I think a lot of adults are still stuck in the mode also.)

Gayle is a loving, kind and funny person. Her laugh is infectious. In spite of her sometimes conflicted life, she was always right in the spirit of what was going on and staying at her house meant long hours of talking. About what, at that age, I am not sure but probably boys.

JANICE

Janice lived on Parkhill Street which was not too far from my house on Douglas Street. The house itself was down over a bank that was kind of steep. It offered a place to lie in the summer that made you feel you were standing up and in the winter good sliding.

Janice had a darling mom and a dad that was in and out, mostly out. Two sisters, one 4 years older and one about that much younger.

Janice and I were the same height (5'2"). She had dark brown hair and a very pretty face (as did all the family). She was the most meticulous person. Never went out in public without every hair in place and make up just so. We were always waiting on Janice. Clothes had to be perfect and therefore sometimes if you were getting ready for a dance or a date it could take her hours to decide all these very important things. Her nose was her only constant complaint. She felt it was too pointy and long. (It wasn't.)

Janice was full of mischief. I knew if I went with her I would eventually be in trouble for some infraction of the rules if nothing more than she would convince me to stay a few minutes longer and make me late home. Laughter abounded with Janice. Always has. Her laugh will stay with me forever in my mind. Janice was madly in love with Hank but he was unable to understand her needs so they were constantly breaking up and making up. It was difficult to keep track of where the situation was at the moment. They eventually married and their marriage was as fitful as the courtship.

GWEN

Gwen and I were old Methodist Church kids. We had become friends back in Sunday School.

Gwen is beautiful!! She gets more beautiful as the years go by. Dark eyes and olive skin, dark hair (naturally curly), long eyelashes and of course a good figure. I will say that all of us had good figures. We all took care of ourselves and took pride in what we looked like. But Gwen it seemed did not have to exert as much effort to get the effect.

Gwen was and has always been the one to listen to everyone and only comment when she had something witty, or important to say. Not to say she wasn't in the flow of things but I think she was a real thinker way back and has never stopped.

Gwen lived on Division Street in a very large old house that sat back off the street. The inside was kind of dark as it had all dark woodwork and built-ins around the fireplace. There were big windows but it seemed dark to me.

Gwen was the youngest of 6. Her father was married to her mom's sister and had two girls, then she died and he married Gwen's mom and they had four kids, 2 boys and 2 girls. Everyone was much older except the one brother who was three years ahead of Gwen and really took good care of her and us for that matter. The other brother I remember some but like all older siblings they seem to go off to school or whatever.

Claude, Gwen's dad had heart trouble. He always rested in the afternoon and if we came to the house we had to make sure he was not resting on the living room davenport before we trounced in and slammed the doors.
We often went in the back door and Gwen's bedroom was off the kitchen and we could escape in there. We were all kind of afraid of Claude. He presented a very stern front. Now Gwen's mom was a kick. She was very quick mentally and spent lots of time talking to us and was very aware. She seemed to always be in the kitchen. I remember we used to get into her canned sauerkraut and eat it cold.

Gwen was very mischievous and we spent a lot of hours on the back hill spying on neighbors and pretending we were government agents. We also were always trying to skirt around

Claude which could be a big job. Sneak through the living room on tip toes.

Gwen's family of course put up a Christmas tree. But Gwen's mom refused to take it down. Said that was not her job. So the tree often was still in the living room way into February and sometimes later. Fire trap for sure, but not until the kids broke down and removed it, did it go. I have a suspicion that Claude finally got mad and ordered it out.

DEANNA

Deanna lived on Chase Street which was about a block and a half from Gwen's and at that time the very best place in town you could live.

Their house was very nice but not elaborate. Deanna's mom and dad were pleasant but a little stiff. I was careful to be on my best behavior in their presence. He was a pharmacist and was a partner in one of the drug stores downtown. Through the years I became aware that her mother was very fun loving and her dad wasn't as unaware as I thought. She had a younger brother. So much younger (six or seven years) that he was hardly in the picture. He was adopted sometime during our youth and I remember him coming but not the timetable.

D as we called her was blonde. She and I had basically the same hair problems being that out hair would not do anything we wanted. Always perms, putting up and fuss fuss fuss. D was fair skinned and a little taller than me, not much. Skinny and as girls always wanted to have large breasts, she was flat. We called her F.E. (fried egg). That was worth lots of laughs.

D was slower moving than the rest of us. She was a very deliberate person and NO unnecessary movement. She was a pretty girl with nice eyes but always wore glasses. Near sighted and glasses were a real problem in dating. Always in the way!

We were worried about how we looked but D would only go so far and then she would say "that's enough. Over and done. No more. Can't do any more." If I was going to say one thing that I admired about her it was her clothes. She always had really nice things. Of course we all did. I guess I just liked how she put them together.

When you put all of us together we were commonly referred to as the "Fearsome Five". We were named that by the boys. We were all for one and one for all. We had good families, morals and we did not drink or do any of the things that a lot of kids get into both then and now. We were envied and hated. We stuck together and we were kind of a pack within ourselves. We were not snobby and we mingled but when it came time to have a party or slumber party it was just us.

Four of us had birthdays in March. Mine the 7th, Gayle, 22nd, Janice 27th and Deanna the 29th. Gwen was a straggler in December. March became a party month for us. We celebrated every birthday in grand style. Always a slumber party at someone's house. It became a choice place to have one at my house because at night we could go out in the store and get anything we wanted to eat. That was a big draw.

Seventh grade was wonderful. We had Mr. Loeschpeck for a home room teacher. He was the basketball coach also and very tall. All the girls were in love with him and at the end of the year we gave him the ugliest tie for a gift. We were all so pleased with ourselves. He made school good.

In the seventh grade I became more interested in boys. There were so many around. It was hard to choose. I have finally gotten the point where men really do not hold much fascination but you must remember back then we were in fairy tale land. You know the one that you fall in love with the boy next door and marry him and live happily ever after in a little house with a white picket fence and have 1.8 children. (I have met some of those .eight people – not pretty.)

My first drooling love was Dwight. There had been a long list of infatuations previously – Lynn, Darrell, Gary but nothing that was real. This was real. This guy was around the school and would be at the tennis court dances (if we were allowed to attend). He was at the swimming pool that summer. Oh, he was so cute.

All of the girls had dream boats we were mooning over and our daily trek to the swimming pool was to get a glimpse of someone. We also started wanting to go to the Teenage Dances and had been allowed to join Rainbow for Girls. Because of joining Rainbow what could our parents say to letting us go to the dances.

Sometimes I got to go if my sister and her date would take me and pick me up. There was no riding in cars with boys yet. At any rate that pre-eighth grade summer was wonderful.

School started and our home room teacher was the football coach and a very good looking, rugged person. He himself had played football and in fact been kind of a star at the state college. He was married though and so we really did not spend much of our time over him.

This was a very heavy year for change. All of us wanted to date. I can remember our parents fighting the issue but we were persistent. I think Janice's parents gave in first. I was finally granted permission to have a date and I was fixed up with a friend of Janice's boyfriend Hank. His name was Jerry. Now my parents knew his parents (you know the routine) and none of us could ride in cars so I spent the night with Janice and went on this first date. He was someone I had of course known for years but dating was something else. I guess we went to the show or a dance and when we came home he kissed me good night.

Of course Janice had been out with her heartthrob, Hank, and there was much squealing and talking when we got home.

Jan's younger sister Collette was always somewhere in the wings, or in the cherry tree spying. Kind of like me in the early part of my life. Collette was out riding her bike one day, just prior to Jan coming home with Hank, and she fell and skinned her knee. Taking matters in her own hands she went home to apply first aid. Jan and Hank came home (walking of course) laughing, talking, flirting, to find Collette with Kotex pad (1950's version – fat-cumbersome) wrapped around her wound.

We have laughed till we cried over the ensuing scene of panic and embarrassment Jan endured. Hank was always so full of fun and had eyes that danced when mischief was afoot, so he of course made life even more miserable for Jan.

No one talked about life cycles then. We pretended it didn't happen. You could be doubled over with pain and you smiled and acted like nothing was wrong. We were so stupid because I am sure it was obvious to the guys that something was wrong when you had white knuckles and turned green!

Once you have broken the date barrier the word gets out. I had a few dates but because of where I lived and I was not allowed to ride in cars with boys, I had to spend the night with one of my friends. It came around to the Christmas holidays and Rainbow was having a big dance. Somehow everything got all messed up. I desperately wanted to go to the dance with Dwight but low and behold Vern asked me instead. I was very upset but I accepted.

I remember this date so well for you see Vern was my childhood sweetheart and my first date with him I didn't even want to go. The family had dinner that night at Margaret and David's house. Margaret and Geraldine were spending the night together and Mrs. Anderson said I might as well also. That made it easier for mom and dad to go home when the party was over. Vern came to get me (walked of course) and we set out. I had a beautiful green taffeta dress with velvet trim.

That date started a rest of the year going steady and a relationship that went on for years. We had a pretty good time but Vern would not leave me alone until I consented to go just with him. I was very busy as an eighth grader. I had been elected cheerleader by now and was elected ninth grade cheerleader just before school was over for the year. I also had dreamed of getting into Drill Team and was selected. Janice was also chosen. Vern could not handle my interest in so many things. His possessiveness led to us breaking up just before school started in the fall and I was again available.

The summer of 1951, my favorite cousin, Duane, and the love of my life was to be married. I hadn't prepared myself for this to ever happen because I was so possessive of him. Being my first cousin and somewhat older than me, had never really deterred my feelings. I was sure I would not like Jane, his fiancé. How could he do this to me. But he did. (Incidentally Jane was a wonderful person whom we loved dearly.) We all made the trip to Clarkston for the wedding and it was a sad day for me. I could not enjoy the festivities because of my not wanting things to change. Duane Married. How would that affect me? What I did not realize was how sick Aunty Stella was and that her life would be over by the next year.

Freshman. What a wonderful feeling. At last a fully fledged high school person. We could now enter the world of before school congregating in the auditorium, have lunch where we pleased and had earned the privilege of being treated as potential adults.

My infatuation for boys did not subside. I was very impressed with the Senior boys as were all the girls in the school. It was not uncommon for the older boys to have become bored with the girls they have already dated and cast aside, so the Freshman girls were the new target. We did not realize that it was just part of the process. We thought we were special.

Now Janice was already going with Hank, who was a Senior. I was pursued by a boy named Cliff and he had a friend, Jim who seemed to eye Deanna. Gayle was still going with Larry (Vern's friend) and Gwen couldn't date.

The gang which developed from the group, which also included Jerry and Ron (Gwen's brother) began to not so much pair off as go in a group. We had wonderful times. I did date Cliff as his steady but we all seemed to have great fun in the large group. Gwen was able to participate because of her brother.

My Freshman year was a fun year. Lots of Rainbow dances, teenage dances, shows, times at the lakes, football games, basketball games, all the great fun things. School was normal except for Home Economics. The girls had to take Home Ec. And we previously (7th & 8th) had an "Old Maid" who was less than inspiring. Then we were given another "Old Maid", Miss Curry who I swear had pinched every penny that ever was and afraid of the world of men. She made us make quarters of recipes, halve eggs, make dresses that didn't show any skin. She also was somewhat hard of hearing. When we would finally get to our kitchens to prepare our measly portion of whatever, we would eat crackers from the store room, throw wet dishcloths across the room and in general try to create fun. Janice was the worst at thinking up trouble. Miss Curry was always confused. She knew something had happened but she could not figure out what. She counted the crackers in the storeroom and knew some were gone but had no idea where they went. Since she had the key to the room and only opened it for class she would question us but of course no one knew anything.

That year I was in the drill team which marched for ball games and parades. The highlight of the year was always the Apple Blossom Festival and the parade. It was very exciting to be a part. We had black pleated very short skirts and sleeveless tops with gold braid and buttons. Pillbox hats to match and white boots with tassels. Very smart. We carried batons and did some twirling but mostly marching routines.

That was the year that Aunty Stella died. She was diagnosed with cancer which in 1951 was not that common. It seemed that she went so fast and I guess she did. It was such an awful time for me. She had been my other mother. Loving and kind and had always been there for me. I am not sure that I have ever had a death that affected me as much as hers. It was also the year that Max who sat in front of me in Algebra and helped me through the class, lost his mother. I felt so sorry for him and yet I was experiencing some of the same things.

The year went very fast and as always graduation was very sad. The group that we had been with that year (boys) were all graduating and we were sure that the next year would be awful. I continued to see Cliff for part of that summer but as those things always do, our paths parted because I needed to go on and he did too. He was unhappy (probably for 30 seconds) but aren't they always.

The summer was filled as usual with the swimming pool. By now I was taking Senior Life Saving in the mornings and just plain swimming in the afternoon. I also worked in the store as usual in the evenings and Saturday and Sunday.

One thing that I failed to mention is that my sister had graduated from high school the end of my eighth grade. She was attending Central Washington University. During my Freshman year I had gone to the college and visited her and was given a taste of college life. Met a lot of her friends which came to our place also. She had lots of boyfriends and they flocked in and out during that summer between Freshman and Sophomore years. I thought I was pretty hot stuff getting to mingle with older guys. There were some girls too.

That was the summer that mom and dad decided we should go on a vacation together. It had been years since our whole family had actually gotten in the car and gone somewhere for a whole week. I, of course did not want to go and I am sure my sister didn't either but the ultimatum was delivered and we went. I had gotten my driver's license that March so I was sixteen and it was such an imposition to have to go on a family trip.

We started out and I believe went to Mt. Rainier and then on down to the ocean beaches and finally to dad's sister's in Salem, OR. We stopped at every roadside distraction and saw all that there was to see. At Long Beach we went clamming (dad,

Geraldine and me) at something like 1:00 a.m. when the tide was out. Mom said we were nuts. It was pitch dark and we had no idea what we were doing. We had a wonderful time, not only that night but the whole trip. Dad was always such fun.

On the way home dad made me drive over Blewett Pass which was the worst crooked, hairpin turns piece of road you could imagine. I was so scared but he would not let me quit. He was wanting me to be able to cope with whatever road I came to and that lesson has stuck with me. I could hardly pry my fingers off the steering wheel when we pulled into home.

My sister drove the car, of course, and we had a lot of excuses for needing it. One was choir practice on Thursday night and the other was church on Sunday. One time on the way home we came around a corner and a huge pig was standing in the road. We almost had a wreck trying to avoid the poor animal that had fallen off some farmer's truck. Another time we were coming home from church when we saw a car careening around the up-coming corner. My sister pulled over as far as the shoulder would allow but the man hit us left head light to his right. No seat belts, only brace your feet on the floor for the crash. I sprained my ankle upon impact, when my high heal turned over. We were able to limp home with the car and I spent months limping around with my bad ankle.

I was elected high school cheerleader just at the end of my Freshman school year. It was Janice, a gal named Helen and myself. Because I was a cheerleader I was automatically taken into Pep Club. Kind of a snobbish group of the elite. We had a marvelous time planning for the year and dreaming up our costumes. It took us all summer to practice and perfect all the new ideas we had. It was such a high flying feeling to be so accepted by your peers. Not that I hadn't always but this was confirmation. I was still in drill team which practiced all summer and then there was swimming and work. A very busy time.

Clothes were a very big "must" to be "in" with the crowd. (Same as it always is.) However, we were very conservative. Skirts were down to our lower calf and if you were among the elite you bought expensive anklets (socks) that were wool with angora tops and color coordinated with your outfit. These special socks were rolled down below the ankle and to complement this look you wore white bucks, saddle shoes (brown only) or penny loafers.

Tops were sweaters or blouses with a small scarf (also color coordinated) or a dickey around the neck. (sometimes both) As we became more sophisticated we took to buying long strands of beads which also were color coordinated. If your skirt was a tight fitting one, you could hardly hobble around!

Being a tried and true Pep Club member, every Friday we wore our uniform to show the rest of the school how special and above it all we were. This uniform consisted of black skirt, white blouse with orange scarf and school sweater. Our school colors were orange and black. I, of course, being a cheerleader as well as Pep Club and Drill Team was allowed to wear my school sweater (black with orange lined pockets) decked out with a "C" in orange striped in black, designating athletic achievement, Pep Club emblem, also orange with black year numbers on one sleeve and my nick name on the other. Being just plain Dorene it was hard to come by a nickname, so I took up Johnny in reference to my last name. Very cool! The pocket of this sweater was adorned with pins of swimming achievements (for which I had many), Rainbow bars, Honor Society pin, and any other significant or insignificant recognition pin you could find.

I can remember in the Fall and Spring being so hot in this outfit, but I would not take the sweater off. It was my badge of honor.

Vern was a Senior. He was the star on the football team, played basketball very well and in general was, I suppose, considered a top catch. I must have thought so also because I again succumbed to his possessiveness. We again went steady. He was kind though and very thoughtful. He always bought me presents and took me to every event. He had the best car in school (46 Ford Coupe) and was generally envied by his peers. He did however, have one very big fault. He could not stop doing naughty things. He thought it was funny to go out with the guys after our date and then come to the house and start knocking on my bedroom window. I found out years later that they drank a lot. (Was I naïve or what?) He also smoked which athletes were not supposed to do, but he did it anyway. He spent his parent's money like water, but I guess they let him. He was charming, witty, and always happy but my parents did not like him. Never did. Begged me not to go out with him. I don't know how they stood it but they came to the conclusion that they should not fight it and didn't. I was however held very tightly to a curfew of 12:30 a.m. Most kids got to stay out till 1:00 a.m. but not me.

I had a very hard class schedule that year. Biology, English, History, P.E., Home Ec. and Geometry. One of the fun things of that year, believe it or not, was geometry. I am one of those people that can memorize all the theorems and axioms and still not know what it is about. Some of it came to me, but for the most part my guiding help through that class was Carl. If it weren't for him I could not have made it through. He sat right behind me and he was one of my classmates that had been in school with me since the beginning. I had known him, but hadn't. You know the person you kind of overlook. I always liked him and wondered why he never asked me out, but he didn't. Just helped me with my geometry.

I have to tell you about Home Ec. Now you remember the two old maids we had, well when we went to Home Ec. this year there was a young, good looking woman who presented herself with confidence. As it turned out she was the wife of the shop teacher and basketball coach. Mrs. Pugh. This was the year that I fell in love with Home Ec. We did things we had never thought possible. She taught us rules of entertaining, wonderful recipes (we made the whole thing). She was fun and interesting and we still talk about that great year in Home Ec.

As I look back on that year, in general it was fun, but there were things that I refused to really see as they were. Vern and Larry were always in some kind of trouble either at school or with the law. In the spring of that year they used to crawl out the windows of the English class room and join us on the fields where we were having P.E.

Also that spring they were caught shooting plate glass windows out of people's houses with a BB gun. Had to go to court and pay for the windows. Again, mom and dad bailed him out. I don't think Larry was actually involved. Just maybe guilt by association. Vern had a quality of finding someone to share his pranks.

That summer a group of guys stole beer from a truck that was parked by a driver's house. I don't remember who all got in trouble for that but just one more thing. At the end of my Sophomore year of school I had been elected Drill Team Leader. This was a dream come true. I was sent to Seattle to my cousin's (Mary Lou and LeRoy's) to take lessons and also Mary Lou helped me to get a beautiful costume made. It was gold sequins with black velvet under the skirt. It was the most beautiful outfit Cashmere had ever seen. I also took lessons from a local gal who was considered one of the best majorettes in the valley. She helped me to create routines and gain confidence to perform in a somewhat respectable way.

The summer was so full because I had also been elected cheerleader for my Junior year and there was much practicing involved. There was also swimming lessons and work.

That fall Vern went off to the University of Washington. He joined the Delta Upsilon Fraternity and began a year of drinking, flunking school and coming home every weekend to check on me. I had planned to have a wonderful free year of school but he would not let me alone. It seemed that without warning he would appear at a function where I was and always when I thought I might have a chance to meet some new person. I really wanted him to enjoy being away at school and for me to have the same experience. He couldn't let go. I guess he didn't have enough confidence in our relationship, which probably would have ended. With my friends and the immense activity load I carried I was able to endure that year.

During that same year he was at the U, I went over to some fun functions. I got to go to hear Tommy Dorsey's band at a wonderful Homecoming Dance. I also went to some football games and subsequent parties that I could have done without. It was an education for me as coming from Cashmere, I had not been exposed to much of the world. I was not aware that people openly expressed themselves in public. Sex was something my world had never uttered, let alone participated in. Probably part of that ignore and it isn't so routine. Come to think of it, the word pregnant was never used. These parties were filled with drinking, boys and girls. I had never had alcoholic drinks outside of my folk's home and was amazed and very uncomfortable.

At last he flunked out of school in the spring and his only recourse was to go into the Army.

Another thing that happened that Junior year that was bad was the Junior-Senior Prom. Deanna and I were elected co-chairmen. Nobody would help us and the whole thing was a flop. I assumed the responsibility for the disaster and really I should not have as the class was responsible and they were not interested. For me it was just one more thing that made the year somewhat miserable.

It was during this infamous year that Toy died. I was so broken up about her death. The years at the store she had been the family mouser and as she got older would wander here and there but always back home.

At Christmas time Vern took it upon himself to give me a dog. Didn't ask my folks or me, just got a dog and to top it off it was a Pekinese. My folks were furious but what do you do. We named him Sam. He was mean and snippy and I can honestly say I did not like that dog. Mom kept it for so many years that I just gave it to her. She somehow had a working relationship with him that no one else could achieve. I did not even like to take care of him when they wanted to go somewhere.

I was sad and very glad the night Vern's folks and I put him on the train for boot camp. At last he was going to be somewhere he could not come home and could not try to control me.

In about February my sister surprised all of us by becoming engaged to a man she had only gone with since fall. Elmer. She had gone out with so many men that it was a real shock for us to have her spring this on us. But mom and dad had an engagement party on Valentine's Day and we started our getting to know Elmer.

I can remember mom and dad were very concerned. He was seven years older than her and so quiet. In fact he was the football coach at Cashmere and I knew him from the school but never dreamed he would be my brother-in-law.

My sister was always called Geraldine at home. That is evidenced by my writing to now. However, everyone else in the world calls her Gerry. I alone called her Ge Ge until my kids came along and called her Aunty Ge Ge. All of my girl's friends call her Aunty Ge Ge and in fact the true label is Aunty Ge Ge and Uncle Elmer said fast with no breath in between. If I refer to her as Geraldine around close friends they do not know who I am talking about. I have reverted back to Ge Ge because for me I don't know who Gerry is!

At times our age difference was a problem for my sister. I enjoyed being around the older kids and getting to go places with them. Thinking back it must have been a burden to always have to take care of me. She has not, to my knowledge, ever complained. In fact she has always exhibited care and concern and the need to protect me. She has been my security blanket all my life – what an awesome task. Through our growing up years we had the usual arguments and fights and I am not sure but I feel that when she got married to Elmer was when I first really realized her true worth. Possibly it was maturity on my part.

It was the summer before my senior year that the wedding was to take place. Elmer's folks were from a little town four miles down the road called Monitor. He had a younger sister who was in my class, Bernice – coincidence – I don't know.

Elmer had graduated from Cashmere as we all had or were going to, but being 12 years my senior had gone to the navy in WWII and then to college at Central where my sister had attended. He graduated, coached and taught until he was hired at Cashmere. He mistakenly thought coming back to roots was a coup.

Ge Ge, about middle of her junior year at college was very undecided about her future and left college to come home and go to business college in Wenatchee. She still had friends at Central and they fixed her up on a blind date with Elmer. I guess it was love at first sight because they were engaged and married in a year. Mom and dad didn't think they should marry. He was too quiet, too old, you name it but as always they gave in. The plans went forward. Mother had to have everything just so. She bought huge lace tablecloths for the church tables, silver candelabra, custom made dresses, trip to Yakima so we could buy the wedding dress at Best's. (Later Nordstrom Best). There were showers and gifts that piled up until they nearly drove us from our home.

They rented an apartment not too far from the school and the wedding took place August 7, 1954. It was a very gala affair and went off as planned. I don't remember much else except that when I went back to school my brother-in-law was my study hall teacher. Strange.

Not too long after they rented a house about 3 blocks from the high school. My sister worked for Uncle Leon and of course Elmer taught and coached at the high school. He followed a coach who left in disgrace but had achieved undefeated football teams. He was loved and hated because Cashmere has an insatiable desire to win in athletics, but they also have what I call the "False Store Front" moral code. You can do anything, just don't get caught because we will turn on you! --- He got caught!

Elmer came thinking he could carry on the tradition but the kids were so depressed about the loss of their coach that there was no way he could get through to them.

He had two disastrous years. I don't remember what the record was, but it wasn't good enough for Cashmere.

During those 2 years, one of which he was married to Ge Ge, I spent a lot of time at their house. It was handy for me so I could be as active in school as I needed and had a place to go between events.

They bought their first dog in this house. Vicky – a Boxer. What a dog. She ate the desert for the after game company ---- got clear up on the counter. She dug huge holes in the back yard that when Elmer's dad drove in, he had to be towed out. She ate a whole ham at mom and dad's, she liked to get under the coffee table and stand up. Did that trick when company was there and everything on the table spewed all over. She ate the heels off all Ge Ge's shoes ----- well Vicky is a story of her own. She had a wonderful personality – gentle and loving. Victory Vale. Vicky was a victory but there was not victory in the Vale of Cashmere for Elmer.

At the end of my Junior year I had been defeated as cheerleader. I am sure it was my demeanor. I had spent a miserable year with all the harassment from Vern. I looked forward to my Senior year. I did not have the responsibility of all the practicing for cheerleader and I could possibly date. However, you remember when we were Freshmen and the Senior boys dated us. In reality I did not think there would be anyone to date so did not give it much thought. I had overlooked the fact that the boys in my class had not really been much into the dating scene. Maybe not mature enough and just kind of group oriented.

What difference did it make as I had Pep Club, Honor Society, Drill Team Leader and my four friends? The five of us were constantly together. In many ways there was a feeling that this may be our last year together and we should make the most of our time. We collectively went to dances, shows, have slumber parties and just enjoy each other's company. It was sad when Janice's parents moved to Wenatchee and she was made to go to Wenatchee High School. We still continued to be close and continued to do everything together even though it was "long distance" (10 miles).

Sometime during the fall in Mr. Brodniak's history class, Deanna asked me to guess who wanted to go out with me. I guessed everyone in the entire class of boys but Josh. Did not even think of him. He wanted to go out with me and was too afraid to ask. So it was that Josh and I started seeing each other.
He was 6 foot something and me 5'2". He was the most gentle Teddy Bear of a guy. Very bashful. I could make him turn red very easily and probably did more than necessary. It was a power trip of sorts. Josh was a very kind person and we had a lot of fun that year. Deanna was going with Ralph and then Ershel and we went on a lot of double dates.

Josh played football and basketball and was the usual high school athlete. That winter during basketball season our team went to

Omak and Okanogan for a game Friday night and one on Saturday. This had been a yearly event and my folks were good about taking us for the weekend. We had a grand time at the Cariboo Inn in Okanogan. My sister went of course because Elmer was the assistant basketball coach; the head football coach and then the head basketball coach was the assistant in football. Make sense? It was so freeing and fun to be in a different place and get to hang out with the guys.

We also went to the district basketball tournament that year and my sister took D and I and another girl. It was exciting to go to a new town and different school and see how other kids were doing things. We had always exchanged with Wenatchee but that was about all.

The Senior Class was expected to put on the "Senior Class Play". This was not an option. Spring 1955. Mrs. Sanford, the English Lit and Drama Coach asked me if I would review 3 plays and give my opinion to the class as to which we should perform. Of course she gave me a couple of duds and then the one she wanted which was "You Can't Take It With You". I of course chose the latter. She was so pleased. I had done a wonderful review job. (I think she had the play all cast and ready to start before my review.) Felling my duties to this project were over and never having tried out for a play before, I went my merry way.

The next week I was summoned to the Principal's office. Nothing new as I was in the office a lot and much involved in student government and activities. Only this time Mr. Fleming said "Why didn't you try out for the Senior Play?" I answered in the only way I knew to answer, "I didn't want to". I can still see the expression on his face. He controlled himself but the veins were starting to stick out and turn a little red. Not a good sign with Mr. Fleming. Then the other shoe fell. He said with clear enunciation, "Mrs. Sanford wants you to play Essie in the play and was very disappointed you did not turn out". I continued to give all the arguments against this idea until he said, "You will play this part. Go see Mrs. Sanford immediately". And so it was that I played Essie in the Senior play and did not know until years later when I was looking in the annual that I had been a lead. I know one thing, I was hated by the girl that wanted to play the part and had taken the time to try out. I must admit I did have a lot of fun.

My senior year was probably the most wonderful year of school. I had the "Fearsome Five" friends and a loyal friend in Josh plus other friends. It was almost too much to see it come to an end.

Graduation night my folks were taken to the front of the crowd for the ceremonies. I walked in with someone to the strains of Pomp and Circumstance but it really is a fog. I know the class sang "Halls of Ivy" for which we had practiced a great deal and then Mr. Fleming got up to give the awards. Now Mr. Fleming was my mentor. He was the kind of person you respected. He was the Principal. I always had a great relationship with him. In fact all through high school everyone made me go ask him for special requests. I was not afraid of him but I knew when he meant business. He was the one that called me into his office in the spring that year and asked me if I was going to apply for college and of course I said yes, but I had not gotten around to it. He asked me where I wanted to go and I said the University of Washington and he did it all. I just one day received an acceptance notice.

Anyway, the awards. I was to receive a special trophy from the Drill Team for all my years of work and help and I also received the outstanding Senior award, having your name engraved on the Pep Club Trophy. This was a huge honor which I never dreamed of getting. Gayle received the Jenny Meyer's Trophy (you know the librarian) for outstanding Senior girl and was one of our either Valedictorian or Salutatorian. I think Gwen was Valedictorian. I don't remember much else because by then I started crying and cried, and cried until when we finally reached the room where we turned in our robes, Josh took me in his arms and held me to quiet me. I can still feel that moment. His large body protecting and comforting me through a time I did not want to face.

I guess we all knew that our lives would never be the same again. All of the carefree fun, the dreams of what we might be were now in front of us to prove. I for one was not sure I was ready. I have always been a dreamer and my life up until now was a dream. I loved most of it and did not want to lose that feeling.

We had an all night party after. I had to go home for a while as mom and dad had people in to celebrate but Josh came with me and then we went to the dance and then changed our clothes and were taken to Lake Chelan for a cruise on the lake in the middle of the night. Then back to Cashmere for breakfast. By then we were so tired that all we wanted to do was sleep.

That did not last long though as Deanna, Gayle, Janice and I had plans to go to Lake Chelan to a friend's cabin. Just the four of us. (Gwen's folks would not let her go.) We promised we would not have any boys there and we kept that promise. Josh asked me what kind of booze I would like and I said gin. I had not ever had a drink in high school except at home which was minimal. I just liked the smell of gin.

We loaded up with our supplies and Jan drove and we went on our way. I drank the entire pint of gin and became so ill that I vomited all night. I have never been able to stand the smell of gin again and I did not drink again until I was 21 and then very lightly. In spite of our drunken party we had fun there. It was just the one night that we drank and then we settled into just exploring and having fun.

When I got home from the last celebration I had to go to Twin Lakes, Idaho for Aquatic School. I was signed up to train for my instructors credentials and the folks and Josh took me. It was a two week stay of very intensive swimming and life saving. Lots of First Aid and days in the water rain or shine. It was exhausting but I passed and came home to teach swimming lessons at the Cashmere pool and life guard in the afternoons. I was in heaven. I had finally attained the goal I had worked for all the years.

It was that summer that as I prepared for college which mainly involved clothes shopping and getting the proper recommendations for Rush, that my relationship with Josh was strained. I was going to another life and he was staying back. He told me he loved me. I did not respond. I loved Josh but not in the way he loved me. I found out myself years later what pain that gives, by not answering. It is the most heartbreaking thing to tell someone you love them and not hear it back. My own father could not say it. I know he loved me but he could not mouth the words. I have had others also who rejected my verbal love. I now can handle it better because I know for some it is not possible to commit to that answer.

The day that mom and dad took me to Seattle to start rush, Josh went along. I was so excited about my new adventure that I am sure I left him empty. I have regretted my actions many times over. I should have years ago said I was sorry but I never did and he recovered quite nicely and married a wonderful woman and was much better off. And so it was that my life in Cashmere, Dryden, Cottage Avenue came to an end. Life would never be the same again. Deanna, Gayle, Janice and Gwen were all going to Washington State. In a way I was about to experience real life for the first time and I was not really prepared. The fairyland I had grown up in would be gone.

Cashmere Valley Record, June 2, 1955 - Single copy 10 cents.

"Attentive Audience Hear Seniors Depict Bright Future" - three speakers, Gayle, Patty and Lyle.

"Town Band to Organize Wednesday"

"Woman's Club Picnic Friday"

"Local Apples Sell at New all Time High" ($11.23 per box)

Ads: Western Store – Dress Special $2.77;
       Nylon Hose – 2 for $1.00;
       Bed jackets $1.00

Part II

CHAPTER 12

MOVING ON

The day I arrived at the women's dorms at the U of W I knew not one person there. I don't know why I chose to go to the University when all my friend went to Washington State. Possibly it was the adventure of doing something different. One thing I do know was that I wanted to be a Theta (Kappa Alpha Theta).

Now we all know that it is suicide to go into rush wanting a certain sorority. But there again I didn't know any better. I knew I was going to be a Theta.

I was assigned a room by myself. It was very upsetting. I was not only alone but I was isolated.

The very first night I found out that another girl from Cashmere whom had graduated from high school a year ahead of me was going through rush. Betsy. She took me under her wing and before I knew it I was meeting all kinds of people and having fun.

In years since, I know of no one who has gone through rush that said it was fun but I had a ball. Every day there were parties and new invitations for the next round and it didn't enter my mind that I wouldn't be accepted.

I was very fortunate. Call it dumb luck or what, but I continued to get invitations to all the houses I was interested in including the Theta's. Not so for others. As time went on I began to realize what was happening to some of those around me, including Betsy. She wanted to be a Kappa (Kappa Kappa Gama). Had her heart set on it. But they dropped her. What a day that was. I will say though that Betsy taught me a lesson on that occasion. She didn't let it throw her for long. She gathered herself together and assessed what she did have going for her and pressed on. When it came down to the final thing of course I received an invitation from the Theta's and Betsy joined the Alpha Delta Pi's. She did more with hers than I did.

The glorious day that I moved my things to the house, I was warmly welcomed by two old friends from high school, Marie and Helen. They no doubt were instrumental in my getting invited. Marie lived on the same street with Deanna and Helen and I had been cheerleaders when I was a sophomore and she a senior.

My folks came over for a reception and the boys from the fraternities all came to see the new pledges and there was so much hoopla that I was completely swept off my feet. People sent flowers and I got encouraging notes from just about everyone. Everyone except Vern. He had written me from the Army saying I should be a Pi Phi. He was cool with his congratulations. It didn't matter because he was not there and I was doing my own thing.

On the other side of the state, Gwen had joined Pi Phi and Deanna had backed out at the last minute because of confusion but next time around became a Delta Gamma. Gayle was an independent and Janice was married. How could I forget Janice and Hank's wedding.

Late in the summer of 1955, in the Methodist Church in Wenatchee, Janice and Hank got married. Hank had been at Washington State for three years and they decided to get married. The plan was that they would both go to school. I don't think Janice went more than a semester.

Now Janice was, as we have already established, a perfectionist. She also had very definite "way out" ideas of what this gala affair should be. Hank was a Beta at WSU so that being a Greek Fraternity and their colors baby blue and pink ----guess what we had to wear? She conjured up these Grecian dresses that were over the shoulder and tied around the middle with gold braid. They were baby blue. She proceeded to buy us all shoes without trying them on because they were exactly what she wanted. They were gold strapies. There was ivy everywhere and I guess the maid of honor (her older sister) wore pink. There were fraternity buddies of Hank's everywhere and as they had a reputation to uphold, were very boisterous and consumed a great deal of alcohol that weekend. I remember that my feet hurt so bad from those shoes that I did not think I would make it through the wedding and then there was a party afterwards. I met Hughy at that wedding. He was a darling boy who was so slick talking that when I think of how gullible I was, it still makes me mad. I was so smitten with Hughy that I thought for sure he was the love of my life (another one). He promised to see me in Seattle the week of some big game and I believed him. Of course I never saw him again.

At the U, I was immediately fixed up with dates. My first was a boy from Wenatchee who had come through the line on reception night and decided he wanted to date me. The routine then was for some upper classman in his house would contact some upper classman in my house and make the request. So it was that I started dating Fred. He was very well mannered, good dresser smooth, handsome fellow that I was swooning over for a couple months until he told me I was ruining his studies and did not want to go out with me anymore. Okay.

The next was a Junior who was very much into student government and vary well thought of on campus. He had approached an upper classman and the arrangements were made for me to have coffee with him. He was incredibly handsome, very learned, pre-med and Jewish. For me that meant nothing. For my parents it was intolerable. I must end the relationship immediately. Well, I had no such plans. I was enjoying my time with Pat. He seemed to enjoy me but his family and his Jewish fraternity finally made him see the light that it was totally inappropriate for him to be dating a gentile. When he ended it with me I was very confused. I had no idea that one religion could not tolerate another. I didn't realize the chasm that was really between us.

But there were lots of fish in the sea. The next one was Louie. Another fix up. He was huge and was an oarsman on the UW crew team. I went to a costume party with him. We were Hershey Bars and I will never forget how he was so fascinated by my size that he kept picking me up and throwing me around. Over his shoulder, whatever. By the time I got home that night I was exhausted. As a result of that night one of his fraternity brothers called and asked me out. It was a rule that you could not go out with two people in the same house unless they agreed or two weeks had passed since the first one had asked you out. Tom was his name and he assured me that Louie did not care. So I took Tom at his word. Well that was a mess. I don't know if Tom lied or if Louie had second thoughts but trouble ensued and Tom and my relationship was short lived. Even the next year when my cousin was at the U and carrying the same last name, Louie mentioned to her how awful I was.

Life in the sorority was very fast and furious. Always something going on. In those days the fraternities serenaded at all hours of the evening and night. We would be rousted out of bed to go sit on the front porch in all kinds of weather to listen to their songs and then we would reciprocate with some of ours. Needless to say we spent a lot of time in choir practice. The whole house. You had to know all the songs and you had better sing your best.

We did go to class. I was a Home Ec. Major. There were only a few acceptable vocations for women. Teaching, nursing, sociology and secretarial. I chose Home Economics education. I did well with the Home Ec. Classes. It was all the others I hated. Like the fact that we had to take physical education. A whole year of it. I first took canoeing, then I thought I could get an A in swimming but wrong. I got a C then I took golf. The golf course was down where now stands a very large addition to the hospital. It was filled with geese and it seemed to rain all the time that spring. Every swing of the club was a splattering of "stuff". What a mess.

After the fall of pledge harassment, phone duty, sneaks that netted us with all our clothes strung all over the house, learning the proper way to do whatever, never wearing pants on the first floor and being passed around from one boy to another I was finally initiated into Kappa Alpha Theta in January. It was wonderful. Something that no one could take away from me.

I had become very close friends with Nona, Nona and Kris. We were always together and plotted our lives in a group arrangement. The first Nona came from a very wealthy family in Spokane. She had attended private boarding schools since she was in Junior High, I believe. She had an aunt that lived in Seattle and had the largest yacht I had ever seen and we were (the whole house) taken on a cruise right after pledging. Also she had a grandfather who had another yacht that was quite large and she took us on a cruise on it in the spring. We were treated royally on both events. I had never been exposed to such opulence. The next Nona came from a farm family up north of Seattle and was more of my caliber of existence. Kris was also from a similar family in

Spokane and we all got along very well. Even though Nona came from a wealthy family, you would never know. She was not affected in any way.

During my numb time or maybe I should say myself centered time, Elmer had secured a job in Yakima at a new school just opening. He and my sister lived in that community for 12 years. He was <u>very</u> successful in his coaching.

In the spring of that year Vern was discharged from the army with an injury. He was declared unfit to serve. He came back to the U. I tried to avoid him but he seemed to be everywhere. As usual I finally consented to go out with him.

I really don't have any explanation for my actions other than as the years have gone by I have decided that it was in my cosmos to give in to him. He was trying to finish the mess he started and seemed to be somewhat settled down. His plan was to go to California to mortuary school in Los Angeles. He convinced me that he needed me to go with him --- that he could not make it if I did not marry him and head for California. I finished only one year of school and I really wanted to go more but something in me made me consent to his persistent request to be engaged.

We were engaged late spring just before school was out and planned our wedding for August 25th. We then would leave for California for the one year course. My parents were very upset. They did not want this marriage to happen. My friends were not real excited and it seemed that no matter what, I needed to do this thing.

It was a terrible day when I left my beloved Theta house. Only years later would I know the reason for this move. After all it was very simple. They are named Andrea and Drue, my two wonderful girls.

CHAPTER 13

MARRIAGE

I went home to Dryden to teach swimming lessons, life guard, work in the store and plan my wedding. Mother as usual took up the plans and it was easier this time because she had done my sister's. There were the usual showers, dress making, flower planning and going to Yakima to get a wedding dress. My friends from all sides would be in the wedding. Nona, Nona, Kris, Deanna, Gayle and Gwen, Ge Ge and my to be sister-in-law. Janice was off somewhere with her husband who was a second lieutenant in the air force.

The pleasantries came and went. We honeymooned up at Lake Chelan because we were going to drive to California and that would be our trip. Our honeymoon was a disaster. Should have been a warning but what was I to do then.

The sad part of this whole thing was I did not have a fiery love for Vern. I was infatuated with him but I can't honestly say that I felt about him the way I have felt about others since.

Gayle and Larry were married September 6th and we left for California a few days later. I'm sorry Gayle, I can't remember anything about your wedding except that I have a picture of D and me pouring punch.

Actually the year in California was great. Vern studied and got all A's. We met friends and had lots of fun excursions. I got a good job in a steno pool that I was quickly taken out of and advanced. Vern had the GI bill and actually we lived very well. It was the first time I got to go to Disneyland. It had opened the year before. Since then I have been many times and have watched the tremendous advancement. We didn't have much money but we would save and go to different places. There is much in California to see and we surprisingly were able to do quite a bit. We saved fifty cent pieces and before we left in July bought our first dog. Chico – a Chihuahua.

The year went quickly and it was time for graduation. I wrote letters to many funeral homes in the State of Washington and we received a reply from a man in Okanogan, Washington. I felt heart sick. Move to Okanogan! But we did.

Much to my surprise, Okanogan was a wonderful place to live. We got an apartment there and by September I realized I was pregnant. I was very upset. I was not ready to have a child. But it was out of my hands.

I spent a miserable pregnancy. I was so sick. I had secured a job, (not knowing I was pregnant) and it was just so hard to keep going. Andrea Dawn was born on April 4, 1958. It was Good Friday and I truly believe God was answering my questions as to why I had done all this. She was the most beautiful little thing. Six pounds and not a hair on her head.

Her birth was not an exceptionally difficult one for me, but it seemed to bring out a way of life for Vern that would simply take him over until his death. He got drunk. He drank for two days and that episode started the remaining fifteen years of alcoholism. I am not sure if it was the responsibility of having a family or just his life in general that set him off. He would have times that he was wonderful. He truly loved Andy, as we nicknamed her.

We were very crowded in the apartment so we managed to buy the house across the street that I had wanted ever since we moved to Okanogan. I loved that house. It was white stucco with pink trim. The yard was very well planted. I did not ever get to furnish it the way that I wanted because we could never seem to pay our bills let alone purchase extras. The family had all chipped in and given us all their old furniture. We could never seem to get much accomplished because Vern worked such odd hours. He was constantly being called out in the middle of the night to go all over the county. I was left with the house, baby, job and the worry of his problems. When he was not working, he was carousing all over the town till the bars closed.

I had grown up believing that when you married you settled down and became a responsible person. I was unprepared for the fact that it was not happening in my marriage, nor was any part of my life as I had thought it would be.

It was Okanogan that we went to see Janice and Hank who were now living in Spokane. They had their first child, a girl. We so enjoyed them as a couple after all the years. It was also during that time that Gwen was married to Pat. She had gone through WSU in three years so she could graduate with him. She always was so smart.

Her father and mother were not able to come to the wedding so we all rallied around her and went for her special day. Her sorority sisters put on a reception for them at the Pi Phi house. They then left for a military life for a while as Pat was graduated and ROTC commissioned I believe Second Lt.

Deanna also got married the next year after Gwen. She married Gerald (Spud) and it was held in the Presbyterian Church in Cashmere. I just remember pouring punch and very little else. (I must have been very good at punch pouring.)

Vern's parents and his sister and husband were very demanding people. They wanted to come to our house or have us come to theirs every weekend. My parents were wanting to see us also and so it was that our lives were torn with company, drinking and working to try to stay solvent. Vern spent at least half of his paycheck every month on booze. I was an enabler for him. I always made excuses, tried to keep the bills paid and entertained even when he did not show up.

I worked the entire 4 years we were in Okanogan. I had one month off when I had Andy. I soon became aware that if we were to keep our heads above water I would have to be the one. I know now that I did the very worst thing for Vern. I should have made him responsible for us. I guess I was too afraid of starving or too proud to go on welfare. So I worked. First at the Medical Service Bureau, then the Farmer's Home Administration. It was made enjoyable because of the wonderful people I worked with. I also had a special relationship with the Okanogan Methodist Church. It was a rock structure (round indigenous) and very austere inside. No fancy windows and lots of elderly people. The first Sunday I went there they were so excited to see a young person they would not leave me alone. Needless to say I was very involved as always and made great friends with fond memories. Andrea was the first baby in years that was added to the cradle roll.

One of the church couples we became friends with had a part Chihuahua female dog and wanted to breed her. We let Chico be the father and they had a darling batch of puppies. We got the pick of the litter which was a chocolate brown male that I named Perro. Chico and the son were such a cute pair until one day in the dead of winter Chico did not come home. We were out half the night looking for him; then in the morning we found him dead. He had been killed by another dog and frozen. I was so devastated. Perro did not know how to live alone and ran out in front of a car and was killed within a week. In this sad episode we got an English Bulldog to start over. She was called Chero. She had some rare lung disease and in sight of about 10 months we had lost three dogs.

I have always been crazy over dogs but felt I could not do any more. But on the 4th of July that summer, we had some friends over for a BBQ in the back yard and this little dog showed up. She looked just like the dog in the comic strip Maggie and Jigs. So we started calling her Maggie. We called all the neighbors, every agency and anybody we could think of and never found her owners. We had that dog for about 10 years.

I became pregnant again but lost the baby. It was in the early stages and I do believe that my general physical condition was so bad that I just could not sustain. The doctor told me to wait and I did, but I was determined to not allow Andrea to be an only child. I am not sure what drove me with that but when I was pregnant again it lasted.

My sister was pregnant also. Their first and only child, Brian.

Vern had become quite belligerent with his employer and his wife. They wanted him to do some work around the funeral home and he simply did not like to work. He only wanted to play and drink. One day when I was about 7 months pregnant he informed me he had quit his job. I am not sure what all happened but I was so at the end of my rope. He left on a trip around the state to find a job and he did get one in Everett, WA. I was truly surprised as I thought he was just out drinking. He had charged our credit cards to the max and the hole we were in grew ever larger. I could not leave Okanogan so he left and went to work for Solies in Everett. As my time to deliver approached, my mother came and stayed with me. The baby was to be born the first week in May but by the last week my doctor said enough and induced labor. Drue Lyn was finally born but not without a struggle. She has been all her life unwilling to give in to someone else's time table.

We could not sell our house and so mom just bundled the kids and me up and took us home with her. We stayed a whole month in Cashmere because by then the folks were out of the store and had bought a large home. Dad had gotten a job with the Department of Labor and Industries as an auditor. The reason he was out of the store was because the highway department decided to make four lanes through the area and it took out the building which was the store. Time to quit anyway. They had worked so many years with hardly any rest.

That was a very busy summer for mom as Drue and Brian were both born, just two months apart. She really had me on her hands and then my sister. Lots of nurse maiding. It was a time when the mother got to rest a little. Didn't have to get up after berthing and go home and milk the cows or go back to work!

During that time with the folks I was really down and out. I had no money, a house that would not sell, a husband that was living in another part of the state and two kids. Vern never took responsibility for anything. He just went his merry way saying everything would be alright.

The Solie's gave us a house to live in but the catch was that they had rented to people that were so dirty that the house had to be dug out and completely painted. It was a huge two story house and Vern and I did all the work ourselves while mom took care of the kids. So it was that we finally gathered our belongings from Okanogan and moved to Everett. Actually Vern was better during that year. He seemed to stay sober and was more interested in the children and being what I called normal. I did not work that year, really was only 9 months. I hated living where we did but we met the young couple next door who became great friends.

The huge house next door was owned by Solies also. Baker Ambulance was housed there and they had a regular dormitory for their drivers. Bill and Theone were housed in the top floor. An apartment so to speak. Bill was a driver and Theone worked for a company that made prefabricated homes.

They had one child, Diane. She was a year younger than Andy. Being so close to us we got together most evenings and played cards. The kids played well together and we could open the windows so if Bill got a call they just hollered over to him.

What a life. But we were actually happier there than we had been.

One of the nice things about Everett was the fact that our house was considered by our family as unfit and so no one came to stay!

Vern decided that he wanted to open his own funeral home. His sister lived in Chelan and she kept telling him that there was a great need in that community to have a decent place. We were dirt poor. Had not been able to sell the house in Okanogan but as usual Vern was not the least bit concerned. I applied for and got a job with the bank in Chelan so I went and stayed with his sister and husband, mom kept the kids and Vern finished an obligation to Solie's. We rented a large old home in downtown and used part of it as our living and the rest funeral home.

Vern was actually helped a great deal by the community fathers. Given jobs that he would be paid good wages, such as janitor for the local doctor but he would always do something to get fired.

The jobs were very open ended. He could do the work when it was convenient but he simply could not be responsible. The business started to grow in spite of him. Of course with me covering for him, and his sister, he was free to pursue his alcohol again.

The saddest part of all this is that he was very good at what he did. We spent seven years in Chelan. Both girls started school there, we were reunited with some old friends from Okanogan – Betty, Carl and Robbie -- and in spite of Vern the business started to prosper. It seemed that the more it grew, the worse he got.

It was during this time that we found out that mom had breast cancer. It started a six year roller coaster of her being very ill and in the hospital and being somewhat okay.

My children suffered so much during that time. I was constantly going to Cashmere and most always staying for the weekend and going back and forth during the week. I really do not know how I survived those years. Vern a drunk and not taking care of business, me working to have money for food, mom sick, kids, bills I could not pay. Vern's folks and busy body sister who relentlessly tried to control not only us but everyone she came in contact with.

My own sister was still living in Yakima by then. Brian and the girls always spent time together and especially since we were at mom and dad's a lot. Dad loved to have them and it helped to keep his mind off mom.

In 1966, ten years after were married I left Vern. I loaded the kids in the only car I could take, 1956 Studebaker, and went home. I could not take any more of the horrible life I was living with Vern.

Vern followed me and promised to be better and of course I went back. A tragic mistake again. My folks were so upset that I went back, but I told myself it was for the kids. And as usual things slowly revolved back to the same old thing.

The day they took mom to the hospital for the last time, after another 8 months of home care given by dad, sister, brother-in-law and myself, plus whatever care givers we could find, my sister and I became hysterical with laughter. We were trying to sterilize the bedroom and bed she had been in and ended out on the back lawn trying to cope with the mattress. It was the relief of the awful situation. We were punchy from the years of mom being kind of okay and very, very ill. I don't know how many times she was at deaths door and rallied. I had spent, prior to the final hospitalization a couple of months driving from Chelan every other night of the week to stay all night with mom. She would not sleep and demanded crushed ice. Dad could not cope. My sister would come on Friday night and relieve us, also I usually would come down sometime during the weekend, so we could plot strategy. Dad sometimes called me when relatives showed up and asked if I would come and fix dinner. By the time they took mom away that day, we were exhausted and simply out of ideas of what to do next. When you let down something has to happen and for us we started to laugh.

We, as always, turned to house cleaning to vent our frustrations. The main objective was the bedroom where mom had been. The house smelled of cancer. I have become aware of that odor since in other illness situations.

We tore into the room and hauled the mattress and springs out in the back yard. Washed and Clorox them and everything in the house. When we tried to retrieve the mattress we couldn't make it come with us. Our energy was spent so we laid on the ground and laughed.

Mom was in the hospital a month before she died. She had a very strong will to live. The night before she died, I was at the hospital with our cousin Duane, Jane and dad. Everyone left the room and I stayed. Mom was lying on her side facing me. She opened her eyes, very alert and said, "Good night Do". I knew I would never see her alive again. Do was an endearment she had called me all my life. The next day before I was ready to return, we received a call from the hospital. She was dead. August 14, 1968. The arrangements fell to Geraldine and me. Again we filled our time with house cleaning, cooking and preparing for the relatives and friends that would descend upon us. The church ladies brought food also and we had 65 for dinner that day. Fortunately it was warm and we could make use of the large yard where we had picnicked so much.

To complicate our lives during the last year of mom's illness, Geraldine and Elmer moved from Yakima to Bellevue, WA, which of course I helped. I do believe it was the hottest summer Yakima had ever had and I drove our van down and we loaded it, their station wagon and their old Plymouth Fury. The movers came and loaded the big furniture. We set out for Bellevue in a parade. I was driving the station wagon, Ge Ge the Plymouth and Elmer the van. The Plymouth gave out just as we turned onto the street where the apartment was that they were moving into. We then drove back to Cashmere to collect the kids and then I to return to Chelan. This all took place just before school started. Elmer had taken a job with the Bellevue School District as Vice

Principal of Sammamish High School. Nice move up but untimely.

My sister and I continued to have to go to Cashmere because dad was in such a depressed state that he was not keeping the yard up or the house. We were afraid the place would deteriorate.

After 7 years in Chelan, by the next spring, Vern had completely killed the business and was totally wiped out with alcohol. His dad offered him a job working for him in his orchards. I hoped it would be a change that would help Vern, so we moved.

We were given a house to live in on the lower ranch. It was not too bad a place and after we painted and fixed it up, it was quite livable. The girls did not want to leave Chelan, but they were excited about being able to have their horses right there at the house. We had bought the girls a Shetland pony when Andy was just about 6 and Drue 3 and we were in the horse business from then on. In Chelan we had to keep them up a canyon at the riding club, so it was not very convenient.

I secured a job at the local high school which was perfect because I had all the same holidays the girls had and summers off. Pay wasn't much but it provided the necessities. Plus I struggled to pay off the debts from the funeral home, which I did. No help from Vern because he continued his drinking. He was a little more careful since he was working with his dad and his parents refused to acknowledge that he had a problem.

My dad was devastated over mom's death. He was living in that huge house alone. It had a beautiful yard. When mom was not able to work in it anymore, my sister and I had tried to keep it up. The situation became impossible. My sister and husband were running back and forth every weekend still, and I was trying to work and go to the house and weed and clean until we sat dad down and said "you have got to sell the house". After two years he finally realized that he could not keep it up because he had no heart for it anymore.

The house had been built in the early 1900's and been in one family all those years until mom and dad bought it in about 1962. It was large and had three bedrooms upstairs that were like going back in time. The one room was just the way my sister and I had left ours years before.

There was a huge porch across the front which faced the park that I mentioned before (the bandstand had long since been torn down). Dad usually slept out all summer.

The back yard was a haven of trees, flowers and was all fenced. You could let the kids out to play with the dogs and did not have to worry.

Next door was Marta Brooks (remember my fourth grade teacher) and her husband. She and mom became very close friends and dad and Sid were friends also until Sid had a heart attack and died before mom.

Much happiness and sadness in that house. Lots of picnics, Christmases, birthday parties, and it was so sad that mom had finally found a place of her own, without all the work of the store only to die. She had it wonderfully decorated as always and mom and dad had a place for all their belongings they had hauled with them their entire lives.

Dad was very big on Christmas decorations. At this house overlooking the park he outdid himself. You know that movie about " Mr. Lampoon's Christmas"? Well, that was dad. Every year he blew all the fuses in the house with all the lights he put outside. He also made wood figurines that were all over the lawn, lighted of course. There was Santa and the reindeer, carolers, and other small animals such as deer and rabbits. He helped Sid make a Nativity scene for his yard. They of course won many prizes for their efforts.

I used to see Deanna once and a while during those years. Occasionally Gayle and Larry too as all their parents still lived in Cashmere. I did not see Gwen until about 1963 when we took the kids for a trip to California and stopped in Reno where she and Pat were. By then she was going back to school to get her Ph.D.

Deanna was in a marriage which I questioned. Spud (her husband) was never available to come with her when I would invite everyone to come to my folk's house, usually during the holidays. It wasn't that he was not likeable, it was a reflection of my own life. It is the same thing, we can see what someone else should do with their life, but we can't get a grip on our own. I could not understand Deanna and Spud's relationship. They had 3 children and he seemed, from what I could gather irresponsible. Gayle and Larry I knew would be together forever. They were solid. Jan had dropped out of sight. We would occasionally get a Christmas card from her, but in general she did not communicate with any of us. We were all concerned but unable to explain at the time. We eventually found out that Janice had left Hank twice. The last time she divorced him. Gwen and Pat came to Cashmere but my visits with her were short, she never seemed to have time to spare. I credited it to her family and understood. I was enduring.

We were all very busy with families, and of course four of us were busy with husbands that were not working out, however we would not admit it. I learned one big lesson in this: "there is absolutely no reward in being a martyr and it is very detrimental to the children".

My sister and I started the painful process of going through the house in preparation for dad moving. Mom had never thrown away anything. We found our old prom dresses, the receipt for the hospital when Geraldine was born (I believe it cost $12.00), the old picnic box which still had the essentials in it, every doll, bottle, dress and shoe we had ever worn. It was so overwhelming. Mom had saved every card that anyone had ever sent her.

We would go through things and throw some away and set some out for garage sale. We took some of the things we wanted. We would then have a sale and start over. I believe we had three sales and hauled and sorted until we got things down to what dad would take with him to the apartment across the park, not 100 yards away. The apartment was owned by Uncle Leon. Makes you feel like you are in a circle and things keep coming around. That is history. World history and personal history. We always come back around.

JEAN

Dad was very lonely and depressed. He and mom had been inseparable for 36 years. He just couldn't get going. He read in the paper of the death of an old friend from years back that he and mom used to "run around" with. His wife (widow) happened to be an old Chewelah girl that dad had known all his life. Jean was a drunk. She was not just an alcoholic, she had passed into a new phase of drunk. It was the reason mom and dad had severed ties with them in the past. They could not stand all the drinking.

Dad, the collector of lost souls called her and she was so needy he could not help himself. He toted and fetched for her and practically lived with her. My sister and I endured hoping he would come to his senses. We tried to talk to him and get him to understand that he was not going to change her. He was sure with the aid of going to church and his influence, their lives would be wonderful. After all she was an old Chewelah girl! How much safer could you get!

Now dad was absolutely a nut over his grandchildren. He loved them possibly too much. He teased them, played with them, gave them pipes to hold in their mouths while driving in the car with him. He taught them how to roll cigarette papers and pretend to smoke them. He called women on the street "Toots" which brought much laughter. No I don't say dad was a good influence on the kids. I don't know how they came out of all of that with wonderful memories of grandpa, but they did. None of them smoked. They certainly were never (that I know of) disrespectful toward others. It blows apart all the things we are taught about child rearing. Dad was alive when he was with his kids, big and little. He was full of stories that he should have written down. I like the one about the canon ball hitting him in the chest during the Civil War, leaving a round red (birth mark) on his chest.

Jean hated children! She and Fred had lived their whole lives doing just as they pleased. Spending everything they took in, and now Jean was left with nothing but a very small Social Security check and my dad who was a sucker for lame ducks.

He came to my house in late November, I believe around 1971 and informed me that he was getting married and since Geraldine and I did not approve we were not invited. There was nothing left to do but wish him well and let him do as he wished. The kids were so upset because since Jean had come into our lives dad had virtually ignored them.

They were married and I was so upset that I don't even know the date. Dad moved to Wenatchee into Jean's house.

Jean did not want any of my mother's things in her house, so she talked dad into selling a Duncan Fife red mahogany dining table and 8 chairs with needle point seats, a beautiful old desk with a fold down writing space, and a bedroom suite all for $65.00 and in the process they bought a davenport, chair and coffee table that was so cheap in looks and workmanship that even a novice could see how utterly sad a "deal" it was. Never a call to us to ask if we would like to keep the items and if $65.00 was all they wanted for them I would have gladly paid. In the antique market it was worth several thousand dollars. The awful man that bought them refused to sell them to me for any price. I think he wanted them for himself.

We spent about 4 years dealing with Dad's marriage. During that time dad was either at my place or Geraldine and Elmer's. He would leave when he couldn't stand it anymore and then he would go back. He would insist that we be invite to things at their house, and then she was so ugly to the kids that I finally told dad that I wanted him to be happy and the best thing for both of us was to not see one another.

During this time of dad's problems, my life was less than wonderful. The kids were having a wonderful time having their horses close by. We spent all summer in the 4-H horse program. Vern and I became 4-H leaders. You might say I became the leader. The kids learned how to show their horses. We had acquired Dan a registered Quarter horse, we still had Smokey, and Drue had an array of horses after she could not ride Smokey any more, and finally settled on Fritz also a registered Quarter horse. We spent from June of 1969 till June 1974 in that house. There were some really good times. I worked as usual trying to keep ahead of Vern. His alcoholism was becoming acute and my endurance was running thin. He was good at telling the girls he would do something and then not showing up. There were a lot of tears over this and I was constantly trying to make excuses for their father.

I began my final run of coping. One day at the high school where I worked one of the male teachers said to me "Dorene what is wrong". I had never before had anyone notice that I was spent. I of course said "Oh nothing". He said he did not believe me and told me to come to his room after school to talk. I did. It was the first time in my life that anyone had really listened to me. I bore my soul to him and he to me. We became friends and confided our problems until I found that I had to tell Vern about this friend who understood me.

A Vern I had never known emerged. Mind you, this was a man that had never in the 25 years I had known him said "I love you". I had never felt an euphoric sensation when I looked at him, in fact I had begun to feel hatred. He accused me of having an affair and proceeded to go up town to all his drinking buddies and tell them as much. In no time at all it was all over town that I was having an affair. I of course told my friend that I would not talk to him again and to please not even speak to me. Over reaction but I was so appalled. Vern also told our family doctor about my alleged activities and made arrangements for me to see a psychiatrist. He said I was crazy and I truly felt crazy so I went. The result of this visit was that I was not crazy. Everyone had a breaking point. I had reached mine. He also told me that Vern was not well, which I already knew. He told Vern as much and this did not set well. He told him he would not help him if he did not quit drinking. I really do not know how many visits they had. I do know it did no good.

I lasted with Vern until after Christmas that year. Living even a more strained relationship with Vern who sneered at me. Sometime in January he came home one night very drunk as usual and proceeded to tell me he was going to kill me. That has a tendency to get ones attention. I ran to the phone and called my sister and she called dad in Wenatchee and sent him up to protect me. There really was no need as Vern fell into a drunken stupor shortly after he chased me down the stairs. My sister and Elmer came in the middle of the night and literally through Vern out.

I stayed in the house until June when school was out. During the time I became very ill and had to be hospitalized. I was a physical and mental mess. My girls were the only thing I had going for me. They kept me alive and going.

We moved to the apartment on Cottage Avenue that dad had lived in. It was a very homey and warm atmosphere and even to this day the girls say that was the best time of their life. Vern was very vindictive. He filed for divorce and as we had nothing but debts we divided them. I really did not know how I was going to make it with two kids and a minimal salary. Vern did not want to pay child support. He thought he could get by with just buying them things they needed. I knew this would not work as he had never paid for anything but his booze for 17 years of marriage I fought for $150.00 per month and got it.

We were dirt poor but I had so many friends who helped me. Gave me food and clothing. My sister and brother-in-law practically carried me. They bought me a car because Vern had sold the car out from under me. I think one of the nicest things anyone ever said to me was "Why did you wait so long". It was the first time I realized that everyone knew what he was. I thought all those years I had hidden it from everyone. When you grow up like I did, divorce was not an option.

In this apartment we had brought with us our dog of the hour, Penny (Fuzz to close friends). Andrea had had a Collie that she showed in 4-H. She was devastated that we could not take her with us. It was just impossible. The dog was on loan from the other 4-H leader and she continued to keep the dog and let Andy show her. She won Grand Champion at both the local fair and the District Fair. The other dog we had was a hunting dog of Vern's and he kept Boggie. The kids were really torn. They would go down to the ranch and clean house for their dad and bake things for him. Sometimes he didn't even come home. They were very upset. He kept the horses at the ranch and they spent that summer riding and he did take them to horse shows. However, I would not let them go unless their grandparents were along. I could not trust him.

That summer he rolled his dad's brand new pick-up and was so drunk that he didn't get hurt. He of course left the scene so he wouldn't be arrested. After that, Andy cried herself to sleep many nights because she was sure her dad would be killed in a car accident.

On the morning of December 19, 1973, my cousins Duane and LeRoy entered the office of the school and said they needed to talk to me. We went to the faculty room where they told me that Vern had dropped dead. He was 37 years old. He had just used up his body and his heart gave out. I was numb.

CHAPTER 14

STARTING OVER

They got Andy out of class for me and Duane went to the Junior High and picked up Drue. They took us to Duane and Jane's house where we told the kids.

It was such a mixture of feelings. Sadness, relief for a person who was destined to be nothing but a drunk, frustration over the years and the past months of divorce and wrangling. I was unable to even grasp what all the possibilities were.

We went home and tried to come to a realization of the facts. I was showered with food and wonderful people who came to me with comfort. That is all except his sister who immediately started her relentless pursuit of finding out who was the administrator of his "estate" as she put it. There was no estate but she simply could not get through her head that she was not in charge. She called every attorney in Okanogan and Chelan Counties trying to find a will. I knew there was no will. He never took care of anything. She proceeded to make all the funeral arrangements, which was fine with me as I really did not feel I had any rights in the matter. She bought the best of everything. Her folks happened to be back east at the time and it took them a couple of days to get home.

When they got home they all came to my house to discuss the matter. It was then that my girls and I were to experience the worst realization of our lives. Vern's folks sat in my house and told us they would not be responsible for us and for us to get the horses out of the corrals at the farm. None of us said anything. His sister invited my children to sit with "the family" at the funeral. We said nothing. I was gracious and even served tea. But when they left we made a pack that we would never ask those people for a thing, since they had made it clear that they were afraid they would have to help us and they were unwilling to do so. My girls have never gotten over this. They have never had any respect for them. Through the years, they were with them only when I made them. When they got older and I really could not do anything about it, they refused to be a part of their father's relatives and simply ignored them. The loss was theirs. These individuals never enjoyed their two granddaughters because they were too busy or too afraid it would cost them money. Everything in their lives has been gauged by money.

We endured the funeral which was a farce. I could not figure out who they were canonizing. It certainly was not the man I had been married to. Anyway it was over.

I again tried to figure out how am I going to live. It was my sister that took me in tow and said "you are eligible for Social Security". It had never occurred to me that this was possible. She took me down to the office and low and behold I was to get more money than I had ever had in the years prior. I was floored. Also the Veteran's Administration contacted me and said that my girls were the recipient of a life insurance policy that Vern had. One that I had paid the premiums on for years. It was divided between them and put in the bank and we did not touch this money as we vowed it was for college.

Also one day at the high school, the Sun Life representative that we had known for years came in the door and asked for me. He presented me with a check for a policy that I thought was expired. It was an annuity policy and it still was worth about $5,000.00 as Vern had not bothered to change the beneficiary so it was mine. I was so overwhelmed with all of this. It came to me that Vern had finally done something for his family. It is awful to say, but his death was the best thing that ever happened to us.

I was able to pay Geraldine and Elmer back the money I owed them and get a good car. I was able to let Andy go to Hawaii with her friend for two weeks and we also went for a two week trip to Disneyland with Ge Ge, Elmer and Brian. While driving all over Southern California we visited all the major college campuses. I was of the philosophy that you talked to the children about when they went to college, not if they went. I tried to instill in my girls that they should be prepared for life. Have a degree.

It was also during this time my cousin LeRoy's girl Cheri got married and her husband was in the army. He was sent to Korea and she moved into the basement apartment below us. She and her sister Chris, who was there most of the time became fun loving companions for my girls. They really helped them through hard times. They would all jump out of bed when the fire siren went off and all run to the car and head for the excitement even if it was in the middle of the night. They had a cat called Puff that played with Penny. If one of us made popcorn the other could smell it and we would congregate. It was a happy time in spite of the death of their father. They did not have to worry about him anymore. One of Drue's best friends lived across the street. Andy had a job after school at the City and we were very happy and comfortable. I should have stayed that way.

My friend from the high school, Ted, separated from his wife and started calling me. In fact, back when I had divorced Vern he had called me. He even gave me money at one time. He was very undecided as to what he was going to do. We basically talked on the phone a lot. I also heard from various old friends (male) some married and some not, but no one I would get mixed up with.

Drue was my safety valve. I would say I could go if she came along. That really discourages men!

An old friend from high school (the one that helped me with my Geometry) Carl, called me and he was living in Seattle at the time. He came over a couple of times and we went out and then I went to Seattle and stayed with my sister and went out with him, but we were just friends.

Ted started getting serious and I was very impressed with him. By now he was divorced and living in Wenatchee where he was working for a school district as an administrator. He was kind, generous, loving and I had never experienced anything like that. Again my fairy tale ideas made me think this was utopia. It was in the beginning. He asked me to marry him. I was so excited. We were going to build a house with bedrooms for my girls and a room for his boys to stay in when they came to visit. It was a dream come true.

In the mean time my dad who had been showing up on both my sister and my doorsteps off and on for 4 years, showed up on mine with all his belongings. This consisted of a coffee table, some fireplace tools, his golf clubs, clothes and a few odds and ends, filing cabinet, typewriter, etc. He was driving an old station wagon he had picked up in a used car lot for a little nothing. He had paid Jean's mortgage for her, and left her all the furniture and his good car. I took him in.

He had to sleep in the living room on the hide-abed but we managed. He was retired by now from the Labor and Industries and truly a broken man. This was about the end of September and Ted and I had decided to get married on December 27, 1975. So we lived like that for three months. It was okay. Dad did on occasion go to Bellevue to be with Geraldine and Elmer.

Ted and I spent time looking for land to build on and eventually found a place at the end of a canyon in a little town between Cashmere and Wenatchee. It was still in the school district that our kids attended and on the bus route. We bought it and he started the very large task of making it livable. We had a deadline of December to move in so it was a lot of effort on all our parts. My girls were very upset. They did not want to move to this place because when we bought it, let me tell you it was awful. An older woman owned it. She and her husband had started building and then he died. She had lived in the basement which she considered finished for ten years. It was the worst dirty, cat ridden, buggy place you could imagine. No one who came there could imagine what we did. Least of all our children.

We completely renovated the basement, added a fireplaces both up and down, and completely finished the upstairs (split level) by December. The yard was nothing but dirt but it was winter so it didn't matter.

We started our life which for me was wonderful. I did not realize what all was going on because I was so intent on this being my utopia. I am not sure how to describe what happened in the fifteen years that we were married. It was really bizarre.
Ted was a workaholic. This is a condition that by some standards is admirable. But he was so obsessed that he worked at his job 10 – 14 hours a day (and was sure to tell everyone how long he had worked) and then came home and worked more.

During the first 10 years of our marriage he worked his job, built a swimming pool with fences and lots of concrete around, built a 40 x 20 solarium, put in a yard, installed a satellite TV, graveled the road, refinished his boat, built a six car carport and God only knows what else. I know one thing, he was always going out in the woods or somewhere to get fireplace wood. I came home one day to find a load of logs dumped in the driveway. We had so much wood stacked around there was hardly any room for anything else. It was a wood obsession along with general obsessiveness in all matters. He also, as an administrator of school activities started having state athletic events which ate up more time. Oh yes, and he went back to school commuting to Ellensburg twice a week for a year to get his Principal credentials.

While he was busy with all that, I was working full time at a demanding new job in Wenatchee, raising his oldest son, Scott, who came to live with us the first year we were married, set Andy off to college at the U of W, tried to go to all of Drue's and Scott's functions, entertained whomever Ted brought home for whatever (sometimes without warning). He loved large functions. His youngest son was with us a good deal of the time and I helped with the State Track meets and tournaments also. Drue had announced one day at the end of her freshman year that she would not go to Cashmere Schools again. She wanted to go to Eastmont. So after getting her out of one school and into the other I started a three year run of taking her to school on my way to work. This was not on my way. And then there was the return trip. Ted was not available to participate in this little ritual as he went early and never came home.

Also during this time dad who had stayed on in the apartment when we moved out, was diagnosed with lung cancer. No big surprise as he smoked his whole life. They removed his bad lung and he was fairly good for about a year when it reoccurred in the other lung. I started the trek to Cashmere after work about twice a week and then three times a week and then every night. Saturday's I would have to clean his place and mine. I had some help with Drue. She was good about it. Geraldine and Elmer would come on the weekends and we limped along. Dad had, since moving back to Cashmere started seeing Marta Brooks, the neighbor in the old house. They really had some great times together and my sister and I couldn't help but wish he had found Marta instead of Jean. They could have had so much.

Dad became dependent on oxygen and had huge tanks in his house. He still drove his car with a portable tank (this was scary) until he got too bad. He used to drive to Wenatchee and take me to lunch about once a week. Never any warning. He always wanted to go to a place called "Sambo's". Loved it there. I went.

He finally got so bad that he asked to be sent to the nursing home. This was a tremendous relief to me. I still went every day, but I did not have to worry about what was happening to him. I had a parade of people checking on him all the time he was alone and it was getting worrisome. So on the first weekend of May 1980 we moved dad to the nursing home. It was the same day that Mt. Saint Helens blew and our world turned black. He would be there until August 6th that year when he died. We had the apartment to dismantle and we did it a little at a time so really by the time he died everything was finished. Dad was very organized in his death. He had everything settled. The money was transferred to us (my sister and me), the car title was signed over to Brian and we had the apartment cleaned and vacated.

The family all came and we had a big dinner at my place and unlike mom it was over. As I think about it now everyone in dad's family is dead except Aunt Ethel and Aunt Valdine. They all seemed to go in a short time. Roger and LeRoy are gone out of the cousins. Uncle Leon is 95 and going strong. Ara, his second wife, died a long time ago. Aunt Emma and Uncle Jake died very close together. Even their son Don is gone. Uncle Walt and Aunt Margaret both gone. Uncle Clark and Aunt Vesta gone a long time ago. Everything has changed. Mom's family all gone except cousins that we never really knew.

After we were married about 5 years I really began to notice a change in Ted. He was suspicious of me, somewhat paranoid and had periods of not communicating at all. I passed it off because when he was "normal" our life was good. Busy but good. He was good about helping with dad and he really was compassionate with me in regard to all I had to do. He often bought flowers and always bought wonderful gifts. We also started going to National Conventions of the Athletic Directors. He first went to San Diego by himself. I was happy for him to get to go and we really could not afford for me to go and with all the kids it was just impossible. In a couple of years we were able to go to Anaheim as Scott and Drue had graduated and had gone on to college. These trips were in December so it worked out well for us. We had good times with a group of people we had a lot in common with. We went to Nashville, TN, Las Vegas, NV, Dallas TX and had wonderful times.

Another problem Ted suffered from was an active case of either hypochondria or Munchhausen syndrome. He was always at the doctors and always had something wrong with him physically. He obsessed about his prostate and even after seeing a specialist who said there was nothing wrong with him he continued to go to a doctor who examined and treated him and eventually operated on him!

He had allergies, back problems (had surgery), aches and pains everywhere, headaches – you name it. He had a knack for making the doctors think there was something wrong, or maybe just realizing a gold mine, and testing him and whatever. The two times I was really sick and in need of help, he left me alone to survive by myself. At any rate it was very tiresome.

Sometime during that 10 year period my Aunt Ethel in Chicago sent my sister and me each $3,000.00. It was so amazing to just out of the blue receive a check for such a sum. Anyway the result was that the four of us went to Chicago. I will probably never have such a wonderful experience again. It was so good for several reasons. They treated us like royalty and we got to know relatives that we had been separated from for so long. Cousin Val lives there also and we spent part time with her and part time with Ethel and Carl. For the first time I found out who Val really was. Enjoyed her immensely. Her husband Dick was a joy to be around and their son Carl so much fun to get to know. It was the revival of my fairy tale life for one week. We went to Chicago another time for the PGA Senior Golf Tournament which was being held at the Medina Golf and Country Club where my aunt, uncle, cousin and husband belonged. We had VIP passes to everything and again were living very high. These two trips gave me a new perspective of Val, and I found a loving aunt and uncle that I had not ever had the opportunity to know.

It was the summer of 1985, my 30th year of graduation from high school, that I received a call from Deanna. We had always talked, not always frequently but off and on. She asked me if I was going to the class reunion. I said no. She was silent and asked why? I said I didn't want to. The truth was that I was not about to go to my class reunion with Ted. He was an awful poop. You never knew if he was going to be nice or awful and chances are that he would be awful since it was something for me. He found great joy in making fun of me when others were around and telling lies about things that he had actually done and saying I had done them. Anyway D. finally broke down and told me she and Spud had been separated for <u>two</u> years. I was screaming at her. "Two years! Why didn't you tell me?" I also told her I was not surprised which she was shocked. I guess it is always the same. You think no one else can see that person you are making excuses for and covering for is a jerk. A drunken, carousing ne'er-do-well who has contributed very little to the family but misery. She was so relieved because she didn't want to go either and face all the inquiring people. I told her she didn't have to go. That phone conversation started a renewed closeness for us which only increased over time.

Ted's illness was progressing at a very rapid rate. Probably the true diagnosis of his problems will never be known for he would never seek help. He was two people. The loving, kind, thoughtful person and the paranoid, suspicious, combative person that followed me to work to make sure I was there, and checked on me every afternoon to make sure I went home. Of course, what I did not know or want to think about was that he was pursuing another woman. That was the way his illness circled. Pursue a woman, marry her and start pursuing another, divorce the first and win the second and then pursue another. He was very combative. We had conversations about nothing. He would list all the awful things I supposedly had done since he had met me. I used to listen to him go on and on and wonder where he had come up with these things. Each episode came more frequently and the list got longer.

Finally in September of the last year, Scott, his son whom he had put down and ridiculed his entire young life, and I decided to seek counseling. I was at the end of my rope and Scott was in dire need of help also. We made an appointment with a counselor and went together. It started a year and a half of probing myself. Learning that I was a good person. Finding out that fixing everything was not going to happen and fool hardy. Within a month, Ted left. It was October 1990. I was so defeated. I had tried so hard to make a go of a second marriage. I was so sure that if I had done one more thing he would have realized we were okay. But it did not happen and through counseling I found out that it never would.

As always my family rallied around me. Fortunately he had left me and not the other way around. I had the house and all the contents which were mine to begin with. I spent three years in that house dealing with all the problems and the severe winters. But I did it. I made changes for the better. Things that I had always wanted to do. I had wonderful neighbors and friends that helped me. My cousins, LeRoy and Duane and their wives were there for me and really it was the beginning of my life. I had made two dreadful choices in marriage and through counseling I found out that marriage is for two people and I had always dealt with only me trying to make it work. I was not bad or unfaithful or wrong or anything. I was a person who had needs also and they were never met through marriage.

The woman I had worked with for 17 years, a dear, dear friend, Mitzi, carried me more than she will ever know. It was so difficult getting up every morning, going to work facing people that I knew had questions, but I was incapable of answering. I couldn't even talk about anything related to my marriage. Mitzi kept me laughing and I am sure covered for me at work. There were times I couldn't remember being there.

My sessions with the psychologist were draining. He taught me to scream. That sounds strange but I had never screamed in my whole life. It was such a wonderful way of releasing all my anger and frustration. He taught me to journal, to talk to people and to accept. There is so much in this life we cannot change. Therefore we must accept and in the process of accepting move on to new things. It was a tremendous struggle to emerge on the other side of a thought process that had been formed from childhood. All those fairytales had to be sorted through and discarded. Real life had to be brought to the front. There are no Prince Charmings. There is no man that is going to take care of me and pamper me. I must stand on my own two feet and do it myself.

My wonderful girls took me to the ocean for a weekend trip, my sister and brother-in-law helped me endlessly with the house. My sister organized the first Johnson Family reunion held in years. I helped some and we held it at the Campfire Camp at Lake Wenatchee. We had over 80 relatives come and it was a huge success. It was held on September 10 & 11, 1990. My divorce was final September 9th. It was good to have something to do and keep my mind occupied.

The next three years I stayed in that house and worked at my long time job. I went to the coast almost every weekend. Football games in the fall, Deanna and I went to the ocean at least twice a year, concerts and family gatherings.

This was the time for D and I to really get back to how it had been in our early lives. We talked and planned trips. Mostly we went on short local ventures. We had a favorite beach and we would go at least late spring and then early fall. We became so close that once again, I could read her thoughts. We spent hours antiquing at every shop we could find. We would pack our car the same way each time. We didn't even have to consult each other as to what we were going to bring. I called her one day, I remember it was spring and said, "Let's go on a fun trip". She as usual said, "Okay." "What do you have in mind." "San Diego", I said. D said, "You plan it and tell me how much I owe." That was the way we operated. I planned, she wrote a check.

We had the most wonderful three days in San Diego. We rented a car and went everywhere. Also, her daughters who happened to be in Los Angeles, came down and the four of us had a fun time.

Experiencing the freedom of travel, by ourselves, aided in our becoming independent. D had worked for years teaching school at a juvenile facility in Tacoma, WA. She was dedicated to kids who really did not have a chance in life. She made a tremendous difference in their lives. She used to tell me stories of what she encountered and the tremendous need her students had.

After probably the worst winter of all time, I suddenly, in January of 1993, got up one day and decided to sell the house. I had thought about it but had not made up my mind until then. I called a real estate agent that was the brother-in-law of the fellow I worked with and by April the house was sold and I was moved out. During those few months, the business where I had worked for so long, was being reorganized and it suddenly became clear to me that I did not want to continue. When they (family) moved my belongings I had them sent to the coast for storage. I lived with a friend for three months and retired from my job on July 16, 1993. It was the most difficult and the most wonderful thing I have ever done. I will never be able to have another Mitzi at my side even though we remain friends. I have so many friends there also. The school wives that stuck by me through all the upheaval. Georgia, Sandi, Carole. Sherrie who had her own problems and yet spent hours hearing mine. My struggle was very hard on everyone. I have so much hurt from the area. I have trouble going back.

I came to Bellevue, WA where my sister lived and found the perfect apartment. I was now within 5 miles of Gayle and D lived about 20. Jan was in East Wenatchee and Gwen in Reno. I was in heaven.

CHURCH

I simply can't go any farther without back tracking a little to tell about my church experiences. Mind you I was brought up in the Methodist Church. We went every Sunday and many other occasions such as work days, pot lucks, weddings, funerals and well you get the picture. I do believe part of the experience is brain washing and part guilt. You know the old "if you don't go to church, blah, blah, blah.

So where ever I was I went to church. You already know about Okanogan. Good experience but let me tell you about Chelan.

The seven years we lived in Chelan almost completely soured me. I was determined to not give up on my church. It was the first and only time in my life that I had a minister tell me I was not a fit person for he and his wife to come to dinner. He, however, used me for his own purposes. I did the bulletin every week, taught Sunday School and worked diligently in the women's group.

The minister left and a new one came who was entirely different and things became much better. During those years Drue would not go to Sunday School unless I went with her so I spent seven years teaching. Both girls were trained in the Methodist Church. Baptized in the church but as a lot of youth, have not been real consistent in attending. Maybe I shoved too much on them.

RETURN TO CASHMERE UNITED METHODIST CHURCH

When we came back to Cashmere in 1969, I of course went back to the church of my birth.

The structure was the same. I was in awe when I entered the sanctuary where the ceilings were so high and the feelings of past overwhelmed me. I was welcomed by those I had known for years (and were related to me). Grace and Clark Bixler were still there, Marie Larse (Larry's mom), Uncle Leon, Duane and Jane, LeRoy and Mary Lou, my cousins, Grandma Dronen's grandson and many more. I felt at home.

I was immediately encouraged to go to Circle, which I did. But there was an odd feeling that I started to perceive. Those that did not know me were skeptical of me. I felt a threat to them in some way. It was difficult for me to comprehend because I couldn't imagine what about me could be threatening. I know now. I was new. New is a possible threat to status quo. New might bring different ideas. I didn't feel new, but I was. I ignored and did my own thing.

Within a year I found myself chairman of wedding receptions held at the church. An honor? NO! A big job with a lot of work that for twenty some years I filled. I soon realized that no one wanted the job. It was okay. I had it organized to such a point that it really wasn't that big a project. Some years there would be 5 weddings and some 15.

I was eventually appointed to the Board of Trustees and subsequently became Chairman of the commission for a number of years. This I enjoyed as we were trying to update the church which had been let go for a long time. There were times though, when they would call me at work to tell me that the roof was leaking and my only response could be, "Get some buckets under the drips. I can't do anything about it right now". I received calls for all kinds of things which I couldn't have fixed myself even if I was there. It became a joke at work as to what calamity had occurred at the church.

I felt proud when I left because we had moved forward with new windows, renovation of the back hall with carpet, Lighting and paint. French doors installed in the Narthex which gave light to the entry and a general enthusiasm for rejuvenating the old building. People started coming forward to volunteer to mow the lawn, plant the flower beds and come for work days where we hauled away 20 years accumulation of "junk" from the entire building. I hope this pride and participation has continued.

CHAPTER 15

LOVES OF MY LIFE

ANDREA DAWN

My first born. There is something about the first one. It doesn't mean that you love the rest any less, but there is such magic about the first.

She was a beautiful baby. Very petite, quiet, good. I kept her in designer outfits and everything was perfect for her. Her room was carefully decorated. She didn't want for attention being the first grandchild.

Vern really showered quite a lot of attention on her. We would take her for sleigh rides in the fresh snow. Always put a cardboard box on the sled where she sat. In the summer she loved to play in the water and smell the flowers.

In Okanogan where she was born, the neighbor next door had a little girl (Holly) a year older than Andy and Fran (the neighbor) baby sat for me. It was a perfect situation.

She had to start with two sets of grandparents, but when Vern's sister had a girl several months later his folks turned to her child and eventually children and never turned back.

Andy was an easy child. I can honestly say she never disobeyed me openly. I know there were many times that she was gritting her teeth, but she never said anything.

When we moved to Everett Andy was three. We became friends with Bill and Theone and their girl Diane; Andy had a new friend. They used to play intently and make the comment that "we are both Diane". Andy seemed to want to be called Diane. Theone and I would take the kids to the park. Andy still talks about those trips.

Drue had been born and she was a serious problem. Cried most of the time and was not a happy baby. Andy spent hours entertaining her as best she could.

Andy started school in Chelan. She was a child that excelled in school. Dedicated to whatever she was doing. She had lots of friends but she had one that was particularly close. Sally. They were practically inseparable. Joined Blue Birds together then Campfire. Went to Campfire Camp faithfully every year. Loved the experience.

Andy was always a child I could count on. During those years in Chelan when mom was so sick, I knew that whatever I asked of her she would do. I was in Cashmere a lot and when I didn't take them with me, they spent a lot of time at their dad's sisters. She was in many ways cruel to my girls. They didn't tell me a lot of what went on until years later, but they endured because of me.

Andy learned to bird hunt with her dad. She went fishing with him and she even started golf lessons because of him. She tried very hard to have quality time with Vern and always wanted to please him.

When Andy was about 6 we bought a Shetland Pony for Christmas for the girls. We kept him at the Saddle Club and Andy loved to ride. It was a difficult situation. We could never leave the phone unanswered because we ran an ambulance service as well as the funeral home. So often Andy was short changed because her dad was off drinking with his buddies and I could not leave to take her. If I had had any gumption I would have just left and let him suffer the consequences instead of the girls.

Andy was in 6th grade when we moved to Cashmere and she was not happy about the move. Drue by this time called her "Miss Priss" because she was so proper about everything she did. It took her a very short time to have a whole new set of friends and be very much in the flow of things. She was a cheerleader during her Junior High days. I think two years. As always Andy was an excellent student and involved in everything she could find the time. She wanted to take piano lessons. I found a way to buy a piano and she began the years of frustration over the fact that she was tone deaf for one thing, and she had to work twice as hard as everyone else and really did not have much confidence in herself. She never excelled but today she can play because she learned to read music and as with everything was skilled.

The freshman year she went to high school where I worked. I was privy to her achievements (which were many) and her hurts. Always proud and marching ahead, Andy went through high school being in everything and graduating with high in her class. She excelled in science and received honors for her efforts.
Andy always had boyfriends. She seemed to attract more than was necessary. Always some or many sitting in my living room or just hanging around. Only once did I have to end a relationship. She thanked me as it was something she did not know how to end.

Andy has always been my rock during very hard times. She is a child that grew up before her time, with her father and his very obvious problems, and then my miserable second marriage. I could always count on her. When her dad died, I know Andy suffered greatly. She had been the one who tried so hard to be a part of his life.

When we came into some money I was able to do more for her. Our new car was a boost. She got her driver's license. I never worried about her with the car. She was totally reliable. She worked after school to earn her own money, something she has never quit.

During the time the three of us lived alone, Andy went to Hawaii with a friend for 2 weeks. A wonderful experience and the beginning of a love for the islands. I also took the girls to Disneyland. Andy did not want to go on that trip but turned out to enjoy it the most. I started a lifelong romance with Disneyland for her.

She has always been a lover of animals. Her two biggest loves were Fancy the Collie she showed in 4-H and Dan her Quarter horse. She won many Grand Champions with the dog and lots of ribbons with her horse. Andy showed her horse until she was a Sophomore in high school. She had to quit because I could not cope with the transportation of the animals alone. We had to board the horses at various places and it became too much. I know these things were very hurtful to her. I wish there was some way I could go back and change what happened. At the time I was so overwhelmed with everyday survival I did not know what to do. I have been very concerned through the years about the damage I did to her and there is no way to change.

When I married Ted I made sure her room was furnished just the way she wanted it because she would only be there for a few months until she went to college.

Andrea Dawn was admitted to the University of Washington and left in the fall of 1976 to go through rush. She pledged Chi Omega. She was disappointed at the time but it proved to be good for her. She spent her four years there, went to Europe on a six week trip with her two very best friends, Jennifer and Sandy and graduated June 1980. It was one of the many proud times I have had with my Andy.

After graduation she could not get a job in her field so she continued to further her education. While working full time she entered nurses training and finally her health gave out and she had to quit. All in all she had about 7 years of college and ended up being an "entrepreneur". Businesses, real estate, jobs, you name it. Always making her own way and thinking up new things. Very ambitious.

She met a man, an Austrian, and fell in love. They had birthdays one day apart and were the same age. Erwin was as ambitious as Andy and together they were a combination to reckon with. He was good for her and to her. They parted in about 2009 and Andy met Jeff and they were subsequently married. He is a very good, stable and generous man and we have all grown to love and accept him into our family.

I have probably not done justice to Andy and I know I have not described her physically. What can I say. I am her mother and I know I see her differently than most, however, I will say that when I am with her all heads turn to stare. She is beautiful. Dark brown, naturally curly hair, beautiful face and about 5'4". She always demands respect.

DRUE LYN

Arrived, May 29, 1961, forced to be born which set the pace for her life. She has always been reluctant to leave a warm, comfortable place.

Her first 6 months were a real struggle for all of us. She cried all night, was prescribed a formula that was far too rich for her and gained way too much weight. I finally took matters into my own hands and put her on my own food regime. It became apparent that she did not require as much sleep as the normal baby and was a family task to keep her awake all day and occupied so that she might sleep at night.

Drue was a very determined child. There was never a "no" said to her that she didn't argue about. She never liked clothes. They bugged her. It was a family watch to see if she indeed had any clothes on at all. I remember one summer in particular that she refused to wear anything but a "Florence Chadwick" bathing suit. I had to wash it at night when she was asleep .

She and her cousin Brian were born 2 months apart and were two peas in a pod. They literally grew up together. Same size (round) and ingenious play mates. They knew what the other was thinking. When they were together they never wanted for things to do.

I didn't allow my children to watch much TV. They always came home, changed their clothes and went <u>outside</u> to play (regardless the weather). After dinner a little TV, bath (which for Drue was an event) and then bed.

Drue started school in Chelan. She was a very timid child when out in the world. It was an odd thing because she was so determined in every other way. In her early years in school she once asked her teacher "Did you know I was here". How sad. Drue always had a way of making you feel sorry for her. She had that lowly waif look until she was a Sophomore in high school.

Drue developed a lifelong friendship with Linda. Her mother and I worked at the bank together and at an early age we traded babysitting and the girls became friends. They joined Blue Birds but neither was very interested. We sent them to Campfire Camp and they didn't like it and never went back.

Drue was my shadow for most of her early life. She always had "sore feet" and wanted me to carry her. She wanted to dress up in funny clothes and shoes and parade around. (Shades of Janet and me). Having Linda or Brian there was a help to me, for when they came she was very busy playing in that other world.

When we moved to Cashmere she was in the third grade. She had a very slow adjustment but finally secured a best friend Jinny. They were inseparable. From then on life was better.

Drue was a good student also. I never had to ask her to do homework. In the third grade she won a writing award called the "Caldecott Award". As she laughs now she wishes her professors had thought she was a good writer.

I can honestly say that school was not real happy for her until she was a Sophomore. She did the normal things, cheerleader, student government, dances, etc. but there was something about her enthusiasm that did not spark until later.

She rode her horse the same as Andy and participated in 4-H but not with the gusto that Andy did. She had her dog Fuzz and she and that silly dog I do believe communicated totally. She had wanted a Hamster but that was not in my realm of caretaking so we talked her into a dog. The dog was often referred to as the "ugliest dog ever seen". The price was right though (free). I cared for that dog until it was 18 years old. She had a great time when we went to Disneyland but I think it was mostly because she was with Brian. They had an uncanny way of reading one another. There way of play was so intense. They had names for everything. Like when they went down to the edge of Phantom Lake close by where Brian lived they called it playing in the "sour ground". Maybe it was sour. I never went down there because they were always bringing back polliwogs and frogs.

Drue loved to swim. She was a fish. I had to put her in swimming lessons at about 4 because she kept walking into the lake right over her head. She went willingly to lessons and was touted as a marvel in with the older kids. The bath tub usually was used by her to keep her skills honed during the off season. Many a night I had to mop the bathroom because there was more water on the floor than in the tub!

It was sometimes hard to read Drue. When her dad died she seemed to take it better than Andy, but I really am not sure. My marriage to Ted the same way. However, in that regard both girls have expressed their feelings since. They both disliked him immensely, but to my knowledge never let it show. They were as usual considerate of me at the time.

At the end of Drue's freshman year she informed Ted and me that she would not go back to Cashmere Schools. She did not want to be Andrea's little sister and be expected to perform and be just like Andy. That happens in a small school. The first child through sets the pace for the rest and no one will let them be themselves.

This was the first indication that Drue was emerging into herself. I really did not believe her but in mid August she said we had better get going on it because she meant business. We did and after much scrambling were able to enroll her at Eastmont where Ted worked. We had to pay tuition, but I felt it was worth it since she had not been a happy school person up to this point.

Drue was a different person once she started at Eastmont. She became happy, enthusiastic about school and in general just had a different disposition. She made immediate friends and became very involved.

She tried out for Drill Team and was accepted. She was in student government. She was Homecoming Princess, turned out for gymnastics, track and tennis. She did not date as much as Andy. Her friends were more into going as a group. When she was a Senior she did start seeing one boy regularly. Ron was a very nice, well mannered fellow that was well liked and I liked also. They seemed to have a fun year. However, he was a Junior so at the end of the summer it was over.

Drue graduated with high grades from a class of 300. She was admitted to the University of Washington.

Drue had worked several summers for the Auvil Fruit Co. packing peaches and nectarines. It was a great place to work and she always made wonderful money. She was friends with the granddaughters of the owner, so kind of had an in. She would continue every summer to come home and work there until she graduated from college.

Drue went through rush and after much indecision pledged Chi Omega where her sister was a senior. They had one year in the house together but each had their own agenda and group of friends. Drue was and is very close with Lael. Actually they even look a lot alike and definitely act alike. First Lael was President of the house and then Drue was the next year. She did the tour of Europe between her Junior and senior year. It was a popular thing to do. She and friends also went to Mexico on spring break. Came back with torn up ankle, bronchitis and Montezuma's revenge, but had a wonderful time!

Drue and Brian graduated from the U of W the same day the same year. Just like they graduated from high school the same year a few days apart. Lucky because one was in Bellevue and the other in East Wenatchee.

Drue graduated college in Political Science and interned with a law firm her last year. When she was out of school she and Lael lived in an apartment with other girls until they got their own place. Drue worked for The Seattle Times and Lael worked for a doctor. Lael wanted to be a doctor and Drue wanted to be an attorney.

After three years, Drue started law school and Lael started medical school. Lael was at U of Nebraska and had gotten married. Drue was still single and struggling to financially afford this added education and the intense studying.

She met Beau at law school. He was a year ahead of her. They have been very close ever since and were married after they both were out of school and had passed the bar. July 31, 1993. Sound familiar? That was the year I sold my house, quit my job, and moved to Bellevue. What a year. Also Brian got married June 12th that same summer. My sister and I thought we might lose our minds with all the preparations. However, we should have expected it as they have always done thing at the same time.

Drue has brought me much joy. The day of her graduation from Law School I sat in awe of her tenacity and dedication to achieve her Doctorate. She went on student loans with little help from me which I regret. She is a munchkin full of life. Her sense of humor is kind of off the wall but on going. Being a Gemini her personality is split. It became so pronounced that to make her realize her demeanor I gave her a second name. Drue is the kind loving person. Doris is shrewd, very intense and sometimes borderline mean. During college she called me one night to tell me she had found another personality which she named Dottie. Dottie was the one that was having so much fun and loved to party. After college Dottie seemed to vanish. She informed me, not long ago that Doris was the attorney! Oh yes, she is 5'0" tall, brown hair and beautiful features. I am sure she has taken the legal profession off guard. She is a criminal attorney and I am sure she has never had to ask if anyone knew she was there!

BRIAN

My nephew has always been a very important part of my life and my girl's lives. They were actually more like brother and sisters. I don't remember at what age we started having the kids spend time at each other's homes alone, but it was early on.

Brian would come to stay when we were in Chelan. One time we were taking a boat trip up lake and were in the process of loading all our gear, dogs, kids and Brian. The most difficult thing was Brian. He was always a quiet child except when he and the girls were playing. At this instance he quietly stood on the dock and watched. We realized that everyone and everything was in the boat but him. I said nicely "Come on Brian, get in the boat. We are going to leave." He stood there. Again, "It is going to be a lot of fun, come on get in the boat." Nothing. Vern was running out of patience and gave a command, "Get in the boat! We are going to leave now." He stood there. The thing that finally prompted his leaping in was when the motor roared and Vern announced, "We are leaving! You can stay on the dock of you wish. See you when we get back." Never again did he have a problem getting in a boat.

Brian always rode Smokey the Shetland pony. He would have on a straw cowboy hat and be bouncing along after the big horses. One of the fun games when we moved to the orchard was going on Safari. Brian found an old Pith Helmet in the shed and always wore it when on Safari. They would gather a walking stick and adventures abounded in the orchard.

When the girls went to his house, they rode the wheels off his fire truck pedal car and played school, store, made recordings on the tape recorder and who knows what else.

Brian and Grandpa Johnson were well matched. He loved, as the girls did too, to be with their Grandpa, enjoying the fun of whatever prank he would dream up next. One birthday Brian gave dad a football helmet. He wore that around to the delight of all the kids.

During the years of mom's illness Brian, Drue and Andy spent many long hours entertaining themselves in the lobby of the hospital. At that time children were not allowed in the rooms as the medical profession was sure they were the carriers of all disease.

Once Geraldine and I were making arrangements for Brian to come for a visit and she felt he was old enough to fly over. They put him on the plane and dad was to meet him in Wenatchee. After the plane was in the air for some reason the airport was fogged in and when they got to Wenatchee they could not land.

The plane was diverted to Ephrata a town about 50 miles away. So dad proceeded to drive to Ephrata. What you must understand the airport in Wenatchee is about 20 miles from town so he had already been on the road for a while. When he reached Ephrata he was informed that they had loaded all the passengers in taxis and sent them to Wenatchee. By now we were all frantic. Here was Brian, probably about 10, somewhere out there in one of those old Checker Cabs with God knows who? When dad finally got to the airport in Wenatchee he was told that they had taken them down town to one of the hotels. More trauma. When he drove up to the hotel there was Brian waiting patiently for someone to rescue him. He had not had any problem with the whole day except he had refused to eat. It did not seem to affect him at all. We have laughed since because my sister was famous for putting a fresh salmon in Brian's suitcase for us to have. This was fortunately one of the times she had not. It would have been nice and ripe when he arrived.

As the years went by and the children all grew older, they continued to have fun times together. Drue and Brian were very close. They seemed to experience everything at the same time and continue to do so even now.

When dad died, we agreed that Brian should have his car. It was a green, Dodge Dart. Not your average college student car but it was grandpa's. Brian named it "The Rat". I guess because it was not in the best of shape. He drove that car for several years and every once in a while a story leaks from Brian's friends about what they did in the Dart. It had a sad ending one night when it was dark and rainy and they slid off the road and it was declared "totaled".

Brian graduated from the University of Washington in communications and is a director for a local TV station. He and Susan were married on that very busy summer in 1993.

SCOTT

I cannot leave out my stepson Scott. He came to live with Ted and me when he was 11 and our first year of marriage.

He had a very bad start in life. He was in need of hands on love and attention. It was very hard to walk the narrow line of a step parent living with the parent who really did not want to be bothered with him. I was not allowed to discipline. That seemed really bad at the time but I think in the long run it made our relationship stronger. He didn't need any negative input; he needed support, encouragement and just plain love.

We spent the 15 years of my marriage together. All but about 4 years he lived with us. He could not read very well at first but after tutoring and lots of day in and day out homework helping he ended up doing quite well.

He loved to hunt and became very proficient in the art through the efforts of a neighbor, Sandy who took him many, many times and also spent hours talking with him. He loved to swim and after we got the pool he would spend lots of time with his friend Tom in the pool. He was a tinkerer. He first had an old motorcycle that was safe because it would never run. He worked on that all the time. Then we bought an equally unreliable Volkswagen Beatle. I don't think there was a part on it that he did not have off, fixed and reinstalled. He sanded, painted, jacked up and redid constantly. I can honestly say it kept him totally busy. He was always working at odd jobs to earn money to sink in his car. I'll never forget the day he started down the road and the whole thing simply flamed out. The electrical system just seemed to short out all at once and the smoke bellowed. He was so upset and I was overcome with laughter. I could not let him know that I was in hysterics.

He played basketball (his love) but was not good enough to make the high school team. Turned to track where he excelled. He was on the relay team that went to State and ended up third. For many years through his growing up he did not have a lot of self confidence. But when he graduated from high school and wanted to go to a community college to enter their airplane mechanics school he seemed to start feeling better about himself. Actually there is nothing he can't do if he just puts his mind to it.

We first were told that he was on the waiting list for the school but I received a call on a Monday saying that if he could get to the school the next day he could start. It was good that I received the call, because if his father had, he would never have gone. I immediately called the place he was working and told him. He was of course shocked and undecided because he had resigned himself to staying home and working for another year. I have always been grateful to Jim Wilson who was the owner of the machine shop where he worked for telling him to go for it. He rushed home, we went to Wenatchee and bought clothes and the next morning he was off. I might add not without a struggle with his father who years ago had decided Scott was not capable of doing anything and did not want him to go because he was sure he would fail and proceeded to tell him. This fact has put a wedge between them that I don't think can ever be erased.

He did very well completing the course and getting his license. He subsequently worked for two different airplane companies dealing with agriculture aerial spraying.

He has had years of strained relationships with both his parents. I have always encouraged him to find a common ground with his mother. You do not have to see everything the way the other person does; you only have to accept them the way they are. I think that has happened. As to his father, I'm not as optimistic.

Scott was my strength in the end of my marriage. He and I had endured so much mental abuse. We went together to the counselor. He helped me get on with my life and I hope I helped him somewhere along the way. He is a man who has a marvelous sense of humor, but is plagued with the past parental abuse. His father told him he was too dumb to go to college. That kind of remark has taken a toll on him.

He is loving and kind. He is handsome and smart. He has since changed professions and became a field man for orchardists. He has a darling daughter from a failed marriage and has found a great life with Brenda. She has been so good for him and they have built a beautiful home together. He is ambitious and creative. I feel privileged to have been a part of his life.

CHAPTER 16

MURDER IN THE CHURCH

It was about 1992, during my time alone in the house, several members of our church became aware of a young woman, Anne, who came to church with 4 little girls. It was learned over a period of time that she was in a very abusive marriage. She was brought to the U.S. from England, through marriage to a local man who was in the service.

As she confided in some of the women it became apparent that she must be helped to get out of this horrible situation. She had no work skills, no money and no relatives in this country.

My cousin, Duane, who owns a number of rentals in town, provided a house for her. Several others gathered furniture and household goods. Others hired her to clean house and even secured a job for her. It wasn't much but it was a start. Her husband was furious and continued to harass her but she was determined to make a new life for herself. She had love and support from her friends in the church. Finally, a divorce was granted. However, he had convinced the judge that she was not stable or financially capable of taking care of the girls and subsequently was given custody of the 4 children. What a horrendous blow. It was such a travesty to see this vicious man have custody of four girls!

As time went on, with Anne having some visitation of the girls and getting back on her feet, she met a man who was also a member of the church and they fell in love. It was a fairy tale come true. Everyone was so pleased for her and felt she deserved this new life and a wonderful person who really respected and cared for her. They were married in the church with most everyone participating in the celebration.

Her husband was changing jobs and had to be out of town for a few days, leaving Anne alone. No one could have suspected or even imagined what would take place.

At around midnight or so the sirens started going off in Cashmere. One right after another. Ambulances were racing everywhere. What was to unfold in the next 3 days was unspeakable in the history of this small town.

Sometimes, no one knows the actual time frame. Anne's ex-husband entered her home and stabbed her to death in her bed, nearly decapitating her. He then drove to Anne's close friend's home and entered, climbing to the upstairs bedroom. When she heard something and sat up on bed he shot her, face forward with a shotgun, in the stomach. At the retort of the gun, her daughters came running and scared him off, also calling 911. He then drove to my Cousin Duane's house and entered walking down the hall to their bedroom. Duane had heard all the sirens and started to get out of bed sitting on the edge. He shot my cousin with the same shotgun, hitting him in the side, then turned the gun to Jane who pulled the covers over her head and he shot her, leaving them both for dead. Duane was able to crawl to his fire department direct phone and call for help. (He was at the time Assistant Fire Chief.)

As they lay waiting for help, they professed their love for one another and acknowledged their wonderful life together thinking all the time they would die.

Anne's ex-husband left and drove to the end of a canyon road and set out on foot. He had left the four girls home alone to go out on this rampage of death and destruction. What we did not know was that earlier that evening he had been seen in the vicinity of the minister's home. He was out of town, luckily, for everyone felt they too would have been attacked.

I was called early the next morning and informed of the night's activities and that Duane and Jane were in the hospital in emergency surgery and at that point no one knew if they would live or die. I rushed to the hospital to be with their children and as the morning wore on a multitude of church people came to join the vigil.

Later that day I was allowed to see Duane. His wounds were somewhat less severe than Jane's because he was turned sideways. He held my hand and said, Well sweetie – what are you doing here"? He had no idea of the severity of what had happened or the depth of my love and concern.

Jane's wounds were to her throat and lungs. Her condition was very critical for a couple of days. She lost her beautiful voice, never to be able to sing again, but she was alive. The other woman had most of her stomach removed but lived.

The manhunt for this desperate man went on for days and finally he was captured. The entire church was in shock. We held a community meeting for anyone involved in this horrible incident. A large group of neighbors, church members, Sheriff Deputies, emergency personnel gathered to come to grips with our feelings and the fact that this had happened in a community where people did not even lock their doors.

Several months later we would have to relive the whole thing with the trial. I only attended the day my cousin and his wife had to testify. It was such an emotional experience to hear them and then see this man sitting there with no remorse whatsoever for his actions. He was given several life sentences, hoping he will not be eligible for parole until he is too old to function.

Something good came out of this nightmare. The children were adopted by the foster parents that took them in at the time of their mother's death. Wonderfully kind people. The church grew closer together and I saw a different attitude toward ourselves and others. Duane and Jane gained a new respect for living now instead of waiting and being more aware of life as it really is has taken a small root in the daily life of the community. Whether it will last is unanswered.

CHAPTER 17

REUNION

We are coming into Reno. Start your engines!

For three days the five of us relived our whole lives. It was as though no time had elapsed. The stories of the past came out. We shared our hurts and happiness of the last 35 years. No one seemed to hold back or hesitate. It was another slumber party. Just one more unbelievable time.

Gwen had been separated for 11 years unable during that time to settle the real estate of their marriage. She had possession of the "Castle", full of antiques, rooms for everyone, grounds abounding, and a place for everything. Can't tell you how much fun it was.

We learned of her struggle to achieve her Ph.D. and in the years of her separation from Pat, he had lived with another woman and had two children. Gwen is not one to show her feelings or emotions, but I know there is a lot of pain connected with all these actions.

She has three children. An accomplished artist who is married with three children. A policeman newly married, and a creative tile mason, married with three girls. All Gwen's children are beautiful like her.

Jan had remarried a wonderful man named Jack. She has three children who are all married with children.

Jan told us of her years of floundering after she and Hank were divorced. For a time she had to give her children up to live with their father. She was not bitter but I sensed a sadness for things that had not ever been. Maybe it is because we all had those same feelings.

Jan's darling mother is still alive but suffering with Alzheimer's. She told of her years at home when she was younger and how her father caroused around and drank. She also expressed pain for having been referred to as an "Okie". They had moved to Cashmere from Oklahoma. We were shocked by these things because we never knew. She had all these years carried these things and none of us realized her hurt. I know we never called her names. But that wasn't the problem. I felt so guilty for never having shared her pain.

Jan had her breasts removed 8 years earlier but was in great shape. Just as particular about herself. Always the last down in the morning but with makeup on and her hair combed. We would all look at her from our bleary eyes and rumpled appearance and say "some things never change".

Gayle is still married to Larry. They have three children; two boys and one girl. They also have five grandchildren. Gayle and Larry are like comfortable shoes. Always great to be with and around. However, there were areas in her life that came out that were painful also. Parental happenings from long ago, substance abuse in the family. Concerns for family members that cannot face reality. Nothing is perfect. We soon learned no one had escaped heartache.

Deanna – separated and divorced for 12 years. She has three children; one boy and two girls. She also has seven grandchildren. All college graduates and in good professions. Deanna did a wonderful job raising her children alone. I think the kids know it. Their father was very much a social person. He had a pizza parlor where he spent most of his time. Liked to be with the boys telling stories and drinking till all hours. Kind of the same personality as Vern. Everything will be all right attitude. Totally irresponsible. Never to change.

I don't think there has ever been a better time in my life as that weekend. So much shared. So much learned. So many years erased. So many bonds renewed and strengthened.

It was finding out you are no different than a lot of women today. We are strong and enduring. We have never lost hope. And now we have surfaced whole and know we can make it.

I went home feeling like a new person, thanks to my long time friends.

CHAPTER 18

THE VALLEY

Having escaped my meager existence in the place I once felt so comfortable, I am able to reflect on reality. Cashmere is only one small part of a valley. Each town is a little different but basically the same. New people move in because they see the beauty and possibly they are never affected by the underlying code which I have named "Mental Incest". It is a need to have everything the same even though the entire universe is changing and opening new and wonderful things. It is passed on to those who chose to stay and live. The very first symptom is the same one that drug users, alcoholics, etc. have. Denial. If you pretend that everything is the same and put the blinders on then it will be okay.

Maybe that is alright for some people. I find it stifling. I want to find out what is happening everywhere and I truly enjoy change. It is an adventure.

The very sad thing about this condition is that even though the blinders are on and denial is in gear, change is happening. Not always for the good.

That is what has happened to this sleepy valley that the core group has refused to recognize. The local paper only prints names of Hispanics in the arrest column; ugly matters have to erupt into something so bad that people from the outside bring it to everyone's attention. I have friends that if I question about events they simply say, "It isn't a big deal". Enter head in sand.

This valley could have stayed the way people wanted if only they would have worked with it instead of ignoring. They have allowed "marts" to drive local merchants out of business; they have not paid attention to zoning ridding huge areas of farms and orchards to build large housing projects. They have refused to acknowledge traffic problems until there is nothing but gridlock. There are things involving attitudes in law enforcement and judicial matters that no one seems willing to deal with. Not your problem, you say. Let the authorities deal with it. And who are the authorities?

I have realized so much in my adult years after I came face to face with what is and not just what I want things to be. All the while I was growing up one of the local bankers was a drunk, many upstanding citizens were having affairs and some were even dishonest! These are everyday things, but in Cashmere they did not exist. That is the difference. After moving away I could see it. Even my friends wanted to believe that nothing had changed. It was hard to convince them that "No they haven't changed. We are just seeing them for the first time".

<u>Time Magazine</u>, November 1995. "The Sex-Crime Capital". An article of unspeakable sex crimes, alleged to have happened in a church in East Wenatchee, by its pastor, his wife and assorted members. The accuser is an overzealous detective who by questioning of children subsequently claiming assaults of such a magnitude that it was easy to dismiss. One child "fingered" 80 people! A quote from the article "Perez (the detective) has abused the children in order to persecute the adults. Anyone can see he is dangerous. It is a wonder Perez got the investigator's job in the first place since he has a history of petty crimes and domestic strife, and a dismal 1989 police department evaluation described him as having a 'pompous, arrogant approach' and said he appeared 'to pick out people and target them'. "
This article exemplifies the concept of ignore, turn your back, don't pay attention and everything will go away. Is there

something awful going on? Yes, but it may not be sex crimes. More likely apathy.

Utopia is dead. Long live Utopia.

EPILOGUE

So much has happened since that first reunion.

Cousin Duane's wife Jane died. She was such a lovely person and we all miss her terribly. Duane remarried a woman named Jewel. Elmer was diagnosed with Alzheimer's. He had a struggle and eventually had a massive stroke and died. He was the strong back bone for our family and the father figure for my girls for many years. In some ways it was good that he did not linger.

Since the first "Fearsome Five Reunion", we have had two more. Jan had a recurrence of her breast cancer and died. We had our reunion in her hospital room and said our good-byes. Oh how I miss her. We all gathered for her funeral and laid her to rest in a beautiful spot overlooking the valley. One of the last things she said to me was, "I really don't feel like I am dying". She was right. Jan will never die because she will always be in our hearts.
One month later to the day, Deanna died. In one week's time she was diagnosed with lung cancer and was gone. She had smoked cigarettes since high school and we had all pleaded with her to quit to no avail. Her death happened the way she would want it. We often talked of not wanting to live sick or be hooked up to anything. She worked with her troubled students until 5 days before she died. As I sat and held her hand that last time in the hospital, I told her it was okay. I didn't want to lose her but I guessed she had more important things to do. Even though she did not respond, I know she heard me.

In that last five years, D and I had gone on several trips together. One to Austria. We talked every Saturday morning when we weren't together. I miss her beyond words and feel such an empty place where she should be. We had planned to go around the U.S. together when we retired. At her memorial service Gayle, Gwen and I read the scriptures. I didn't know if I could do it but the needed strength came to me. The minister read letters from her students she had received those few days in the hospital. She had meant so much to them.

Gwen is finally divorced. When she came up for Deanna's service she told Gayle and me. She is now the legal owner of the "Castle". Since she lives in Reno we don't get to see her as much but keep in touch. She seemed relaxed and finally at peace with the situation. She has found a companion whom she spends time with and travels some. She seems happy in her life.

Update: Clark, Gwen's companion was diagnosed with cancer and died with Gwen and her family caring for him and by his side. I flew down and helped her with the arrangements for feeding the family that descended and gave what moral support I could.

I go to Reno at least once a year and try to get Gayle to come with me when possible. Since Larry's death Gayle has found a companion that she is very happy with. All the 52 years that they were married gave her a positive outlook for having another relationship.

These five women have been the main stay of my life outside of my family. A glue so to speak. We have always been there for each other. I know now that much of my life has been made better for having them as true and loyal friends.

These women have taught me that love is not some earth moving experience that comes over you when a man pays you attention. It is care and concern for another person be they man or woman. I know that most men simply can't give an unconditional love and now I am at peace with not looking for that thrilling experience.

If sex is what you are after you can get that anywhere. But true friendship with or without it is the only truly rewarding thing in life. I am blessed. I have, and always have had it.

There will be another reunion next year.

Now there are three.

ACKNOWLEDGEMENT

A special thanks to Terri without whose help this would not have been finished. And thank you to Beau for providing the cover photo.

www.ingramcontent.com/pod-product-compliance
Lightning Source LLC
Chambersburg PA
CBHW051756040426
42446CB00007B/392